T0306048

The Neurodiversity Handbook for Teaching Assistants and Learning Support Assistants

This highly practical book supports the knowledge and development of teaching assistants and learning support assistants (TAs/LSAs) in their understanding of neurodivergent pupils.

Considering a neurodivergent world is vital in society today, and even more so in the classroom. Starting with a model of difference rather than deficit and highlighting the complexities involved, this accessible resource focuses on effective strategies to support these pupils and explores the vital role of learning support in a range of different contexts. Rich in pedagogical features, this book includes chapter objectives, areas for the reader to reflect upon, links throughout to the Teaching Assistant Standards, and case studies for the reader to examine. Each chapter also has a further reading section, which includes links to articles, websites, and organisations that can aid and support the development of TAs and LSAs.

This important work will provide Special Educational Needs Co-ordinators (SENCos) with a framework to support their support staff in the classroom.

Dr Sarah Alix has worked in Education for nearly 20 years. Sarah has experience across a range of settings including schools and universities. She has a Doctorate in Education, a psychology degree, and postgraduate qualifications including the SENCo award and PGCert in Autism. Sarah has a great personal awareness and understanding of neurodiversity through her own family members.

The Neurodiversity Handbook for Teaching Assistants and Learning Support Assistants

A Guide for Learning Support Staff, SENCOs and Students

Sarah Alix

Routledge
Taylor & Francis Group

LONDON AND NEW YORK

Designed cover image: © Getty Images

First published 2024
by Routledge
4 Park Square, Milton Park, Abingdon, Oxon OX14 4RN

and by Routledge
605 Third Avenue, New York, NY 10158

Routledge is an imprint of the Taylor & Francis Group, an informa business

© 2024 Sarah Alix

The right of Sarah Alix to be identified as author of this work has been asserted in accordance with sections 77 and 78 of the Copyright, Designs and Patents Act 1988.

All rights reserved. No part of this book may be reprinted or reproduced or utilised in any form or by any electronic, mechanical, or other means, now known or hereafter invented, including photocopying and recording, or in any information storage or retrieval system, without permission in writing from the publishers.

Trademark notice: Product or corporate names may be trademarks or registered trademarks, and are used only for identification and explanation without intent to infringe.

British Library Cataloguing-in-Publication Data
A catalogue record for this book is available from the British Library

Library of Congress Cataloging-in-Publication Data
Names: Alix, Sarah, author.
Title: The teaching assistant's neurodiversity handbook / Sarah Alix.
Description: Abingdon, Oxon; New York, NY: Routledge, 2024. | Includes bibliographical references and index.
Identifiers: LCCN 2023026065 (print) | LCCN 2023026066 (ebook) | ISBN 9781032548074 (hardback) | ISBN 9781032548067 (paperback) | ISBN 9781003427599 (ebook)
Subjects: LCSH: Teachers of children with mental disabilities—Training of—Great Britain. | Teachers' assistants—Training of—Great Britain. | Children with mental disabilities—Education—Great Britain. | Neurodiversity.
Classification: LCC LC4625 .A55 2024 (print) | LCC LC4625 (ebook) | DDC 371.14/1240941—dc23/eng/20230914
LC record available at https://lccn.loc.gov/2023026065
LC ebook record available at https://lccn.loc.gov/2023026066

ISBN: 9781032548074 (hbk)
ISBN: 9781032548067 (pbk)
ISBN: 9781003427599 (ebk)

DOI: 10.4324/9781003427599

Typeset in Galliard
by codeMantra

Contents

Author Biography

Dr Sarah Alix has worked in Education for nearly 20 years. She works for the Sigma Trust in Essex leading the teacher training provision. Sarah has experience as a youth worker, a primary school teacher and a behaviour support advisor working with primary, secondary and special schools, and working for a university as a Senior Lecturer and Deputy Head of their Education Department.

Sarah has a Doctorate in Education, a psychology degree and many postgraduate qualifications including the SENCo award, PGCert in Autism, MA in Education, and PGCert in HE. Recent publications include *The Neurodiversity Handbook for Trainee Teachers*, researching autistic trainee teacher experiences and a handbook for foster carers. She is a school governor across multiple schools and enjoys a focus on supporting special educational needs and disabilities development in schools.

Sarah is also a Senior Fellow of the Higher Education Academy, a graduate member of the British Psychological Society and a Fellow of the Chartered College. She is part of the Autism Education Trust Expert Reference Group and Schools Reference Group.

Sarah has a great personal awareness and understanding of neurodiversity through her own family members who are autistic, have attention-deficit hyperactivity disorder, dyslexia and general anxiety disorder, and through her own diagnosis of autism as an adult a few years ago.

Sarah has a strong belief that education is where it all starts and that the school years lay the foundation for everything else to come; whether this is to work in health, finance, the arts, business or education, to name a few, it all starts with the building blocks of school. This is why it is so important to promote the acceptance of differences and to begin with this here with support staff. Great teachers, with a secure understanding of how to adapt the curriculum for everyone, will make the difference to thousands of individuals each and every year.

Acknowledgements

After writing the *Neurodiversity Handbook for Trainee Teachers*, I thought it was really important to write a similar book to support TAs, LSAs and SEN-Cos. I would like to thank Routledge Editor, Alison Foyle, for her support and guidance along the way and Rhea Gupta for her work on the chapters. I would also like to thank each of my children, Charlie, Morgan and Maximilian, for being the unique individuals that they are. It is important to thank everyone who has supported and helped me to write this book, given me insight and had discussions with me to form the case studies. This includes experienced staff from the Sigma Trust, SENCos, learning mentors, parents, TAs, neurodivergent adults and all pupils past and present who have had difficulty gaining recognition and the support that they are entitled to as a neurodiverse learner.

Alix, S. (2023) *The Neurodiversity Handbook for Trainee Teachers*. SAGE Publications.

Introduction
How to Use This Book

This book is a practical support book for teaching assistants (TAs), learning support assistants (LSAs), their teachers and their Special Educational Needs Co-ordinators (SENCos) in developing an understanding of neurodiversity in the classroom. This book covers both primary and secondary age ranges and phases within mainstream schools.

This handbook supports the understanding of neurodiversity with the use of supporting strategies for TAs and LSAs; it considers a model of difference rather than deficit that will be explored in Chapter 1.

The chapters move through key areas to support neurodivergent pupils:

They begin with introducing some of the basic areas for development for an TA/LSA in grasping how to adapt the classroom for neurodivergent pupils, behaviour management and neurodivergent pupils, well-being, and the assessment of neurodivergent pupils. It will finish with taking a look at working in different formats and working collaboratively.

There are links to the Professional Standards for Teaching Assistants throughout the book. The Professional Standards focus on four key areas or themes for TAs/LSAs:

- Personal and professional conduct
- Knowledge and understanding
- Teaching and learning
- Working with others

This book will provide opportunities to develop in these key areas, which will be highlighted at the beginning of each chapter.

The book combines theory and supporting knowledge development and strategies on what TAs/LSAs need to know, and what and how to implement their knowledge and strategies to support neurodivergent pupils. It provides guidance on working with class teachers and SENCOs to ensure that they are covering relevant areas of the Standards, Code of Practice (CoP) and their own development towards working with neurodivergent pupils.

DOI: 10.4324/9781003427599-1

The chapters draw upon expertise from Lead SENCos in schools across the age phases, TAs/LSAs and higher level TAs (HLTAs) and personal experiences from a range of neurodivergent people.

The book supports TAs/LSAs at different times of their career as a new TA/LSA in post, establishing their place in the classroom as a developing TA/LSA, or embedding their practice as an experienced TA/LSA in relation to neurodiversity.

The book contains four types of interactive features throughout:

1 ***Reflect*** opportunities for the reader to reflect on the areas of practice
2 ***Professional Discussion*** for the reader to have with their class teacher, mentor, line manager or SENCo
3 ***Activity,*** an opportunity to find something out or seek further information
4 ***Case Studies*** demonstrating examples of practice for reflection or discussion

The book links directly to areas of the Professional Standards for Teaching Assistants and the Education Endowment Foundation's Guidance Report: Making Best Use of Teaching Assistants.

Key Documents Referenced Throughout This Book

The Professional Standards for Teaching Assistants: this is a document written by an independent panel that was formulated by the Department for Education (DfE) in 2016. It consisted of Union representatives and educational experts, and the panel were tasked with clarifying roles and responsibilities of TAs and the workforce.

The Standards are not compulsory in school, but they are strongly recommended by the teaching unions to be implemented and adhered to within schools. Although the Standards were developed in the UK, they highlight the core values and skills for the TA and LSA roles, and can be applied in settings internationally. Therefore, this text is applicable in its use across the globe.

The second key document referenced within this book is by the Education Endowment Foundation: Guidance Report: Making Best Use of Teaching Assistants. This evidence-based report was written in 2021 which focused on studies looking at best practice of the use of TAs.

What Is the Difference between a TA and an LSA?

There are many similarities between the two roles, and often the terms of the two roles will be used interchangeably. It is always best to check your contract and the role that you will be undertaking in your individual school.

A TA will tend to work across the whole class offering academic support to all pupils and being a good role model to them.

An LSA will often work 1:1 with pupils and may have a pastoral role, and a supporting role with the implementation ofinterventions.

However, as I have said, often the roles are interchangeable, and this book is valuable for both roles, including HLTAs, and for SENCos to use to support staff in schools.

Reflect

What have you heard around the term 'Neurodiversity'? What does it mean to you? Where have you heard it and when?

What do you already know about special educational needs and disabilities (SEND) in schools? Is this different to neurodiversity or not?

1 Introduction to Neurodiversity

What Is Neurodiversity?

Chapter Aims

- To gain an understanding of the neurodiversity model and how this differs from other types of models for special educational needs and disabilities (SEND).
- To gain an overview of the main forms of neurodiversity that you may encounter within a mainstream school.
- To consider the importance of positive attitudes towards neurodivergent pupils.
- To ensure understanding of the use of inclusive language when working with neurodivergent pupils, considering a model of difference rather than deficit.

Links to the Professional Standards for Teaching Assistants

Personal and Professional Conduct

- **5 Committing to improve your own practice** through self-evaluation and awareness.

Knowledge and Understanding

- **1 Acquire the appropriate skills, qualifications and/or experience** required for the teaching assistant role with support from the school employer.
- **2 Demonstrate expertise and skills in understanding the needs of all pupils** (including specialist expertise as appropriate) and know how to adapt and deliver support to meet individual needs.
- **3 Share responsibility for ensuring that your own knowledge and understanding is relevant and up to date** by reflecting on your own practice, liaising with school leaders and accessing relevant professional development to improve personal effectiveness.

DOI: 10.4324/9781003427599-2

What Is Neurodiversity?

As humans, we all acknowledge how similar we are, for example, how we look, how we behave and how we live our lives. We also acknowledge the physical differences that we see, such as our hair colour, our height, our weight and even our socio-economic backgrounds, including where we live, what job we do and what possessions we own.

But what about the differences we can't see? What makes us unique in our behaviour or how we process things, including how we learn, how we react and how we sense things?

This chapter is going to examine a model that you may not be familiar with and will begin to give you an understanding of the terminology and paradigm shift in thinking towards neurodiversity and pupils with SEND.

We could present the argument that everyone is neurodivergent in their own way. For example, everyone has individual differences in how they process information and how they respond to this. This is as unique as our fingerprints. In schools, the education model is designed to accommodate and teach to the broadest category of differences, that of the 'neurotypical' learner, which accommodates 60%–85% of the population. This is the learner that fits into the majority of the population, and therefore the easiest to accommodate in terms of their learning within a class with 30 children and a broad model of education.

Let's break the term 'neurodiversity' down. It was first used in the 1990s and means

Neuro (neurological) – meaning the nervous system, the brain

Diverse – meaning differing from one another

Judy Singer was a researcher in autism, and she adopted the phrase in 1999 when discussing autism in her writing. The field of autism research and support is where it has grown in usage since, and has then been extended into other neurodivergent areas and the many forms of the neurodivergent brain, and includes people with attention-deficit hyperactivity disorder (ADHD), dyslexia and many others which we will examine later in this chapter. Singer (2017) wrote about neurodiversity in an academic context, in which she explored the difficulties that autistic communities faced.

There are many studies on neurodiversity which indicate that in the UK there are approximately between 15% and 20% of people that are neurodivergent. The rest of the population is classed as neurotypical. However, depending on the study conducted, it is thought that potentially up to 30%–40% of the world could be classed as neurodivergent in some form and sit outside the neurotypical framework of learning and processing. These figures don't include people with extreme forms of intelligence and giftedness such as savant syndrome and hyperthymesia (extensive autobiographical memory) which, it could also be argued, is a form of neurodiversity. This shows the potential of how wide neurodiversity could be.

There are three main types of model in which we see being implemented within society today: the medical model, the social model and the biopsycho-social model. We will look at each of these further.

The Medical Model

The medical model is currently the model that has been in place for decades within our schools. It is a model in which everyone who fits into the majority in the way that they learn is seen as being 'neurotypical'. The medical model implies that there is a 'right' way of functioning and processing, which is the model in which the education system is built around, and which you yourself would have grown up being educated within. It implies that anyone who processes information differently, therefore, has something wrong with them. These pupils are seen to have a deficit or an impairment, or be described as having a disorder. These 'impairments' are seen to fall short of what is a normal, neurotypical cognitive way of learning.

The medical model 'aspires towards normalization, symptom reduction, and elimination of conditions based in deficits to cause functional impairment in life activities' (Kapp, Gillespie-Lynch, Sherman and Hutman, 2013). The aim of the medical model is to alleviate the symptoms of the disorder and to get rid of any symptoms or the unwanted behaviours so that the person 'fits in' to the expectations and 'norms' of the neurotypical population. Rolfe (2019) argues that the medical model believes that any deviations from the neurotypical population and expectations are an impairment within the child that needs to be addressed.

Neurodiversity is key in challenging this model; it does not believe that there is a right or wrong way to function, or for cognitive processing, they are just different for different learners. The medical model is socially constructed by neurotypical learners, and the neurodiversity model aims to deconstruct the medical model and begin to view learning and individuality differently and as equal. Slorach (2016) argues that these differences in cognitive functioning are part of natural human variation, just as other elements of human development and difference are. It is normal to have variation within our species.

The Social Model

The social model outlines a collective responsibility by society to support and address any difficulties that have been created by how a society is formed. Rolfe (2019) argues that it is because barriers are created by society, and that this then, in turn, causes the barrier to become a disability, rather than addressing the need and adjusting the environment so that the person can function within society.

The Biopsychosocial Model

The biopsychosocial model is built upon a combination of both biological and social elements. It is based upon to understand a person's medical condition; it is both the biological factors and also the psychological and social factors and their complex interactions that need to be considered to gain full understanding of the issues and the impairment.

The neurodiversity model challenges each of these three models above. Instead, it argues that 'difference' is not a disability itself, however, the way in which the social context, the environment and the interactions that have all been formed and valued by a neurotypical society are what cause discrimination.

Consider human characteristics such as eye colour. Did you know that around 75% of the world's population have brown eyes? Approximately just 10% have blue, 5% hazel, 5% amber, 3% grey, 2% green, 1% red and 1% different coloured (WorldAtlas, 2022). Is there a right and a wrong coloured eye type to have? Should we fix eye colour so that everyone's is brown? Just as our eye colour is different, obviously so are many other human characteristics: skin colour, hair colour, height, body shape and fingerprints. Our brains are different too: how they are shaped, the size of them and how the pathways may join or form slightly differently.

Instead of thinking 'disorders' or 'impairments', we need to make a shift in our own thinking and understanding to know that different processing is normal, natural and ok! The neurodivergent brain works differently to the neurotypical brain, similarly to how a computer using Microsoft or/and Apple processing system might use different ways to get to the outcome that is needed or the difference between an Xbox or Playstation to play a game.

Is Neurodiversity the Same as SEND

Sort of, but it is the use of terminology and viewpoints that differ. A SEND model in school focuses on what pupils can't do (compared to neurotypical people) and closing a gap, whereas neurodiversity focuses on celebrating natural differences in the way in which everyone thinks and learns, focusing on strengths and adjusting the environment so that it suits neurodivergent people too. Neurodivergent people may have educational needs and may have disabilities associated with the barriers that they face.

In schools, a medical model is generally currently still used, and it is a way of identifying neurodivergent pupils. However, moving to a neurodiversity model in which we focus on difference rather than deficit will have an impact on pupil self-esteem and well-being, and it will promote a model of acceptance of a normal set of differences which should be respected as all other differences such as gender, race and culture are respected. Recognising difference as a natural variation should be implemented, with the knowledge that what might work for one pupil won't necessarily work for another.

Labels and Language Used. What Does This mean?

The Diagnostic and Statistical Manual of Mental Disorders (DSM) criterion is used as the assessment criterion for many neuro-differences. We are currently on version DSM-5. Each area of the manual covers neuro-differences and the criteria that need to be met for a person to be given a diagnosis. It covers areas such as autism and ADHD, and over the course of the rewritten versions, areas have changed and developed as research has become greater and we are becoming more knowledgeable around neurodivergence. For example, you may have heard of 'Asperger's syndrome', which is no longer in DSM-5; it has been removed and the criteria for this are covered under the broader umbrella of autism.

There are many arguments for and against the labelling of conditions or neuro-differences. Labelling can be viewed with negativity as it can be seen as limiting, or pre-judgements about a person could be made. Others may argue that through identifying a difference and 'labelling' it, specific successful support or strategies can be implemented.

There is some debate around the use of terms such as disorders and conditions, but the terms are commonly used. The neurodiversity paradigm is not aiming to get rid of the use of diagnosis or labels, or to downgrade them or then dismiss the challenges that people face. There are useful elements to gaining assessment outcomes and identifying labels, for example, to understand the differences of the challenges that someone may have and how they might be supported. Therefore, I have created an overview of the most common neuro-differences below, and there is further reading on many of them in the links at the end of the chapter.

It is important to remember: although neurological differences can indicate challenges which may lead to a disability, they do not indicate a flaw. Neurodivergent people are not broken, are incomplete, or need changing; they are human with natural variation, and society needs to change to accommodate this 20% of our population.

We will be looking at/an overview will follow on:

- Attachment disorder
- ADHD
- Auditory processing disorder (APD)
- Autism (autism spectrum disorder (ASD)/autism spectrum condition (ASC))
- Development language disorder (DLD)
- Dyscalculia
- Dyslexia
- Dyspraxia
- Foetal alcohol spectrum disorder (FASD)
- General anxiety disorder (GAD)
- Oppositional defiance disorder (ODD)
- Obsessive-compulsive disorder (OCD)
- Pathological demand avoidance (PDA)
- Post-traumatic stress disorder (PTSD)
- Rejection sensitive dysphoria (RSD)
- Sensory processing disorder (SPD)
- Tourette syndrome (TS)

Attachment Disorder

Children with attachment disorder will have difficulty in forming attachments and deep emotional connections with their caregivers. This lack of attachment, or weak bond, will have an effect on the child's development. Attachment disorder commonly occurs when a child has experienced some sort of trauma or abuse or if they have been moved around homes and been unable to form secure attachments with their primary caregiver. Children with attachment disorder will have a difficulty in forming connections with others or developing trust which can affect relationships as they become adults.

Children with attachment disorder may become hypervigilant of their surroundings, and the behaviours seen can be similar to a child with ADHD (discussed in Attention-Deficit Hyperactivity Disorder section). They may not seek out comfort if they become hurt or distressed, or they may do the opposite and seek out anyone including strangers, which could put them at risk. The brain develops differently in the connections that are formed and schemas that it makes when faced with trauma, particularly when a child is young and the brain is developing based on the experiences that they may experience. The differences in how these pathways are formed can then impact on how a child reacts to situations and can show as challenging behaviour (Newman, Sivaratnam and Komiti, 2015).

Attention-Deficit Hyperactivity Disorder

ADHD is one of the more commonly recognised and diagnosed neurodivergent differences. It can have similar presenting behaviours to other complex conditions such as attachment disorder or PTSD, so careful diagnosis is needed and then the possible underlying causes of these are addressed if this is the case. ADHD is often diagnosed in childhood, but continues through adulthood, and is more commonly being diagnosed in adults too.

Children with ADHD have difficulty paying attention and will present with behaviours such as fidgeting, making mistakes, losing things, being overactive or having impulsive behaviour and be more willing to take risks. These elements can then impact on adult life and may cause difficulty in maintaining healthy relationships, with a person's self-esteem, or achieving their educational potential.

There are three types of ADHD:

- Inattentive presentation: the difficulty in paying attention to tasks or to follow instructions.
- Hyperactive-impulsive presentation: the difficulty in sitting still or taking turns.
- Combined presentation: the combination of both of the above presentations.

ADHD has a high percentage of co-occurrence with autism.

Auditory Processing Disorder

APD is the difficulty in processing sound and what is being said; it is not a hearing loss. However, people with APD may have developed coping strategies similar to someone with a hearing loss to support them, such as lip reading, avoiding places with too much background noise or avoiding particular situations which could potentially be difficult for them. APD can be more difficult when a person is feeling stressed, overwhelmed or tired. It is a common co-occurrence with other neuro-differences such as autism, ADHD and dyslexia.

Supporting a learner with APD might include repeating information to them, ensuring that they have time to process this, not giving too much information at once, staying focused on the piece of information, slowing conversations or instructions down, reducing background noise and distraction, using written summaries or captions or sending a text or email rather than having a phone call.

Autism (ASD/ASC)

Autism is not an illness but a processing difference. Some autism groups may suggest that autism is something to be cured, but this is not true; it is a neuro-difference. These differences can, however, impact a person's life and pose challenges when coping with daily life and society.

There are three main areas of difference for autistic people: *communication* – in the way autistic people communicate, interact, use language or develop relationships. *Sensory processing* – in the way in which autistic people experience sensory stimuli differently to neurotypical people. They may either be hyper (high) or hypo (low) sensitive, and this can fluctuate for each person, either throughout the day or depending on the environment or task. *Flexibility in thinking* – autistic people are more comfortable with routines and structure that make them feel more secure and safe. Changes to this can cause challenges for an autistic person. They may also have a strong focus or hyper-focus or special interest that goes beyond having a hobby. This can be a real asset.

Other writers suggest further categories or a breakdown of categories; there is a really interesting article by Lynch (2019) in *NeuroClastic* at the end of this chapter on autism, which outlines a broader spectrum of challenges.

It is important to gain an understanding of the use of the term 'spectrum' when relating this to autism, as it is greatly misunderstood. It is often thought of as a length, and someone is either at one end or the other, one indicating being on a higher end and the other the lower end. However, this is not the case at all; instead, it is a profile of abilities, and each individual may be affected in different ways within different categories. This is why we refer to knowing one autistic person is very different to knowing another autistic person. The *NeuroClastic* article mentioned above gives good examples of this in detail and is a key read.

Developmental Language Disorder

DLD relates only to the difficulty in speaking and understanding the spoken language. It is not linked with any other conditions, and normally children who have this have no other conditions. DLD can have a negative impact on a child's education, and it is really important that early intervention and support is sought and implemented.

Dyscalculia

Dyscalculia is a specific learning difficulty associated with mathematical aspects of learning. Often, it is specifically linked with arithmetic and can impact on a person understanding number facts and concepts, and it will affect the fluency and accuracy in making calculations. Dyscalculia can be co-occurring with ADHD, dyslexia and/or dyspraxia. This is because they are likely to share cognitive functions for the processing that is needed to carry out calculations.

Dyslexia

The British Dyslexia Association (BDA, 2010) adopts the definition of dyslexia which outlines that dyslexia is a learning difficulty that affects accurate and fluent reading and spelling. This consists of difficulties in phonological awareness, verbal processing speed and verbal memory. There may be co-occurring challenges in areas such as language, motor skills and coordination, calculations, concentration and personal organisation. There may be co-occurrence with dyspraxia, autism, ADHD and dyscalculia.

Dyslexic people may also have particular strengths in creative areas such as entrepreneurship, design, interaction and social skills and problem-solving.

Dyspraxia

Dyspraxia is classed as a developmental coordination disorder (DCD) and affects fine and/or gross motor skills and coordination in both children and adults. Difficulties may present differently for individuals and may also change over time depending on contributing factors such as the person's environment or life experiences and challenges. Dyspraxia can have a challenging impact upon a person's everyday life skills and also within education and employment.

These challenges may include difficulty with self-care, writing, using equipment, sport or activity such as riding a bike. These challenges can continue and transfer into adult and will be replicated in tasks such as home maintenance, driving a car, organisation, time management and planning.

It is thought that dyspraxia is a neurological difference in the way the brain processes information and transfers the messages from the brain to movements that are needed to be performed.

Foetal Alcohol Spectrum Disorder

FASD was previously known as foetal alcohol syndrome. This occurs when a foetus is exposed to large quantities of alcohol when they are in the womb through the mother drinking excessively. The alcohol is passed from the mother, through the bloodstream to the foetus, and can affect the development of the baby causing issues with functions such as problems with vision, hearing, balance and coordination. Alongside this there may be complications and learning difficulties with memory, concentration and impulse control. These may affect education, and a child could present with challenging behaviours or behaviours similar to ADHD, attachment or PTSD. There may also be speech and language delays, social skills and self-regulation. Further to this, physical complications such as bone, joint and muscle development including organ damage to the heart or kidneys may be present.

General Anxiety Disorder

Life can put everyone in challenging circumstances in which they can experience anxiety at some point, for example, sitting exams, attending medical appointments, job interviews or starting a new job. These are all normal situations where anxiety may be felt by an individual. GAD is when anxiety goes beyond these normal situations and is felt in a person's everyday life, with a daily struggle of battling this anxiety and it affecting how they live. It is a long-term condition, and the daily worries are uncontrollable and will cover a large range of issues and challenges throughout the day.

GAD may have links with other conditions in some circumstances such as panic disorder, phobias, PTSD, social anxiety disorder or autism-specific anxiety.

Oppositional Defiant Disorder

This is classed as a behavioural disorder which is diagnosed in childhood. All children get upset, become irritable and push boundaries at times, which is normal behaviour, but children with oppositional defiant disorder (ODD) demonstrate further challenging behaviours such as defiance; lack of cooperation; negative attitudes towards peers, teachers, professionals and authority figures; and intense and frequent irritability. These behaviours are more frequent and intense than normal childhood and adolescence boundary challenges, and they can impact on positive and healthy relationships with peers and adults and impact on education.

Behaviours that indicate ODD can include excessive arguments with peers, parents and teachers; the constant questioning of rules and boundaries and refusing to comply with them, even if it puts them in danger; blaming others for their own mistakes; becoming irritated and annoyed by others around them or demonstrating what appears to be temper tantrums.

Sometimes it can be difficult to separate what elements are ODD and what are other differences such as autism, ADHD or bipolar, and these differences may coexist with ODD, with only around 10% of ODD is a stand-alone condition or diagnosis.

Obsessive-Compulsive Disorder

OCD can be split and then linked into two parts. The first are unwelcome thoughts which are intrusive and can take over the normal thoughts which can cause anxiety – these are the obsessions. The second are the repetitive actions that a person does to try and reduce the anxieties that have been caused by the obsessive thoughts – the actions are the compulsions. The compulsions, which are the repeating behaviours can take up a great deal of time in someone's day, or a person may avoid particular situations that may be a trigger for the obsessions and compulsions. This could be as extreme as not going to school or work or visiting family and friends. This behaviour can lead to exhaustion for the person and isolation.

Pathological Demand Avoidance

PDA is different to ODD; sometimes people can get mixed up with the terminology.

It is normal for us all at times to avoid certain 'demands' on us, something we need to do or somewhere we need to go to, for example. PDA is when these demands become too much and impact on daily lives. When a demand is asked of someone, this is avoided because someone else has asked it and can lead to a feeling of lack of control or anxiety. At times it can appear to be irrational or over-dramatic in relation to the demand or request that has been asked of the individual. The presentation of PDA can be of either a person showing outward behaviours such as becoming controlling or the use of physical aggression, or the opposite and aperson withdrawing or showing signs of increased anxiety. Other people may have a combination of how they present depending on the environment that they are in and the demand being made at the time.

There is a form of demand avoidance linked with autism: autistic demand avoidance in which the avoidance behaviours are triggered by areas of the autistic person such as sensory overload. Here the person may avoid activities so they do not have to experience a sensory overload, or they may withdraw, refuse or experience a meltdown. To reduce autistic demand avoidance, removal of sensory triggers such as noise or lighting may be beneficial or planned support with any changes or preparation for an activity may help participation.

Post-traumatic Stress Disorder

PTSD is when a traumatic experience has happened to an individual, and a high level of anxiety occurs from this. It could relate to an individual incident or a prolonged period of trauma. The person may experience flashback to the event or events or have nightmares which relive it. Alongside this they can re-experience the fear and anxiety that they had at the time. PTSD is an acute stress reaction; it can cause physical pain, intrusive thoughts, aggression, hypervigilance and irritability. The hormones triggered cause a fight or flight response when one is not needed.

Rejection-Sensitive Dysphoria

People with RSD are over-sensitised to the feeling of being rejected. Most people can feel rejected if they do not get a job that they wanted or by friends at some point, but people with RSD have a stronger emotional reaction to this or to any negative comments that are made to them and feel judged and criticised. This can have an impact on daily life with the feeling of discomfort or failure, or that people are against them that are disproportionate to what is actually happening or taking place. People with RSD may try to overcompensate and people please which can in itself be exhausting. RSD can coexist with ADHD.

Sensory Processing Disorder

We all experience sensory processing. This is a neurological process in which information is taken from our senses, and then passed to working memory where we decide whether to respond to the information or ignore it. The senses include smell, taste, touch, vision, sound, movement, awareness of body position and gravity. Neurotypical people use the sensory information effectively for the environment that they are in or that has been created. But for people with SPD their daily life can be affected through associated difficulties with SPD, which may impact on their education, work, behaviour or relationships.

Individuals with SPD may become hyper (over) sensitive to the sensory information such as having a fear of heights, disliking food textures, having a fear of loud noises or strong smells or disliking the feeling of touch through hair brushing, teeth cleaning or having a shower. A person with SPD may become hypo (under) sensitive to the sensory information instead and may not feel pain or the temperature. They may seek out sensory experiences such as the need for rocking or chewing things. Both hyper and hypo can be interchangeable within an individual and can alter throughout the course of a day. SPD is often co-occurring with autism and ADHD but can also be a stand-alone neurodivergence.

Tourette Syndrome

TS is a neurological condition that is inherited. It affects about one in every hundred people and mainly affects boys. Involuntary sounds and movements known as tics are presenting behaviours with TS, and in a minority of people with TS, coprolalia in which a person swears or says inappropriate things occurs. However, this is not a common aspect of TS although most people think it is. TS can co-occur with other neuro-differences such as OCD, ADHD and anxiety.

Co-occurrence

In the above explanations of the neuro-differences, co-occurrence is often mentioned. For example, 60% of autistic people will also have ADHD, and autistic people may also have anxiety or sensory processing differences. This is where labelling can be useful to identify where there are differences and where there are overlaps and what supporting strategies may be beneficial.

Developing Positive Attitudes towards Neurodiversity in Society

There has been a shift in language from the use of, for example, 'autism **awareness** day/week/month' to 'autism **acceptance**'. This is a really important shift of language for neurodiversity. We don't just want everyone in society to be aware of a neuro-difference, but we need (and have the right) for society to be accepting of neuro-difference and to ensure that everyone has the same rights and opportunities, regardless of whether they are neurotypical or neurodivergent. We see acceptance in other areas of difference such as gender and race, and we now need to ensure that neurodivergent individuals also receive acceptance as part of society. Everyone has the right for any difference to be embraced and to be treated with dignity and respect.

The current model in society expects neurodivergent people to change, to be more sociable and to fit in with a set of norms that have been implemented by neurotypical people. In effect, it is similar to asking other minority groups to dress differently to be accepted. It is highly prejudicial and discriminatory, and it is not acceptable.

There are many areas in neurodiversity in which further barriers need to be broken down around acceptance. This can be associated with the stigma that disability may hold, and some ethnic minority communities may be reluctant to seek support because of this. In other areas, there is underdiagnosis of girls and women with autism and/or ADHD. Many women are discovering later in life that the struggles that they have faced are associated with neurodivergences such as these, which have not been diagnosed, and they have not had the understanding or support for. Much more research is needed in areas such as these; for example, new ways of assessing girls and women are currently being developed. They are important areas to ensure that you continue to read about and update your knowledge on.

Use of Language: Identity-First versus Person-First Language

Different sets of people believe that either identity-first language or person-first language should be used in relation to certain neuro-differences. This is debated within communities of people such as the autistic community. For example, there is a majority within the autistic community that prefers to be called 'autistic' rather than 'person with autism'; they refer to themselves as 'being autistic'. They see autism as being an inherent part of themselves, not as something separate, something added on, or something that they have that they want to get rid of, which is associated with a medical model. They see their strengths, challenges and differences as central to their identity. However, many professionals and parents may refer to someone as having autism and use person-first terminology as they feel as though it should be the person first, and that their difference should not define them.

Tensions lie within the argument, and it is important to consider how the individual themselves would prefer to be addressed, ask them or listen to how they address themselves.

Chapter Summary

This chapter has begun to explain neurodiversity, what it is, the model that represents neurodiversity and its importance when compared with traditional models such as the medical and social models that we see within education and general society today. The chapter directs you to begin to think about a model of difference rather than deficit, which you can then apply when working through the following chapters. The chapter has given an overview of some of the terminology used and explanations of some of the more common neuro-differences or labels that are used.

Glossary of Key Terms

- Neurocognitive – the processes that take place in the brain, for example, the way in which we remember and retrieve information.
- Neurodivergencies – the different neurodivergent strands grouped together.
- Neurodivergent – the way in which our brain works in a neurocognitive way is in a smaller percentage of the population (often having a diagnosis such as autism, ADHD or dyslexia).
- Neurodiverse – a group of neurodivergent people with a range of ways of functioning and processing.
- Neurotypical – the way in which our brain works in a neurocognitive way is within the largest percentage of the population, and society standardises this as 'normal'.

Useful Websites and Links

- Attachment disorder
  HelpGuide: https://www.helpguide.org/articles/parenting-family/attachment-issues-and-reactive-attachment-disorders.htm.
- ADHD
  ADHD Foundation: https://www.adhdfoundation.org.uk/what-we-do/training/.
  CDC: https://www.cdc.gov/ncbddd/adhd/facts.html.
- APD
  Nationwide Children's: https://www.nationwidechildrens.org/conditions/auditory-processing-disorder.
- Autism (ASD/ASC)
  NeuroClastic: https://neuroclastic.com/its-a-spectrum-doesnt-mean-what-you-think/?fbclid=IwAR10zTutk4JTgRoLhTWdNEBRhbw4ch46Y5iKrDWjLFkGb7C1GMgV56f16fk.
- Autism Education Trust: https://www.autismeducationtrust.org.uk/.
- DLD
  British Dyslexia Association: https://www.bdadyslexia.org.uk/dyslexia/neurodiversity-and-co-occurring-differences/developmental-language-disorder-dld.
- Dyscalculia
  British Dyslexia Association: https://www.bdadyslexia.org.uk.
- Dyslexia
  British Dyslexia Association: https://www.bdadyslexia.org.uk/dyslexia.
- Dyspraxia
  Dyspraxia Foundation: https://dyspraxiafoundation.org.uk/.
- FASD
  Foetal Alcohol Spectrum Disorder Network: http://www.fasdnetwork.org/.
  https://nationalfasd.org.uk/.
- GAD
  Mind: https://www.mind.org.uk/information-support/types-of-mental-health-problems/anxiety-and-panic-attacks/anxiety-disorders/.
- ODD
  LANCUK: https://www.lanc.org.uk/related-conditions/oppositional-defiant-disorder/.
- OCD
  OCD-UK: https://www.ocduk.org/.
- PDA
  Pathological Demand Avoidance Society: https://www.pdasociety.org.uk/what-is-pda-menu/what-is-demand-avoidance/.
- PTSD
  Mind: https://www.mind.org.uk/information-support/types-of-mental-health-problems/post-traumatic-stress-disorder-ptsd-and-complex-ptsd/about-ptsd/.

- RSD
  Psychology Today: https://www.psychologytoday.com/gb/blog/friendship-20/201907/what-is-rejection-sensitive-dysphoria.
- SPD
  The Sensory Seeker https://thesensoryseeker.com/sensory-processing-disorder-in-the-uk/.
- TS
  Tourette's Action: https://www.tourettes-action.org.uk/67-what-is-ts.html.

Further Reading

- Autistic Advocacy (2022) https://autisticadvocacy.org/about-asan/identity-first-language/ [date accessed 20.02.23].
- Edinburgh University. About Neurodiversity; How Neurodiversity Can Shape Our Experiences, and What You Can Do to Embrace Neurodiversity. https://www.ed.ac.uk/salvesen-research/about-neurodiversity.
- Is the Diagnosis System Undermining SEND Support? TES. https://www.tes.com/magazine/teaching-learning/general/send-support-schools-diagnosis-system-undermining-send-support-neurodiversity.
- Keeping Children Safe in Education 2021. https://assets.publishing.service.gov.uk/government/uploads/system/uploads/attachment_data/file/1014058/KCSIE_2021_Part_One_September.pdf.
- Lynch (2019) NeuroClastic. https://neuroclastic.com/its-a-spectrum-doesnt-mean-what-you-think/?fbclid=IwAR10zTutk4JTgRoLhTWdNEBRhbw4ch46Y5iKrDWjLFkGb7C1GMgV56f16fk.
- Neurodiversity as a Strengthening Point for Your Team and Our Society. Forbes. https://www.forbes.com/sites/forbestechcouncil/2021/08/13/neurodiversity-as-a-strengthening-point-for-your-team-and-our-society/?sh=5236528d28f9.
- SEND Code of Practice (2020 Updated Version). https://www.gov.uk/government/publications/send-code-of-practice-0-to-25.

References

British Dyslexia Association (2010) https://www.bdadyslexia.org.uk/dyslexia/about-dyslexia

Kapp, S., Gillespie-Lynch, K., Sherman, L. and Hutman, T. (2013) Deficit, Difference, or Both? Autism and Neurodiversity. *Developmental Psychology*. Vol. 49. No. 1. P59–71.

Newman, L., Sivaratnam, C. and Komiti, A. (2015) Attachment and Early Brain Development – Neuroprotective Interventions in Infant–Caregiver Therapy. *Transitional Development Psychiatry*. Vol 3. No. 1 https://www.tandfonline.com/doi/epdf/10.3402/tdp.v3.28647?needAccess=true&role=button

Rolfe, S. (2019) Models of SEND: The Impact of Political and Economic Influences on Policy and Provision. *British Journal of Special Education*. Vol. 46. No. 4. P423–44.

Singer, J. (2017) *Neurodiversity: The Birth of an Idea.* Judy Singer. Amazon Kindle ebook.

Slorach, R. (2016) *A Very Capitalist Condition: A History and Politics of Disability.* Bookmarks Publications. London.

WorldAtlas (2022) https://www.worldatlas.com/articles/which-eye-color-is-the-most-common-in-the-world.html [date accessed 26.05.22].

Reflect

Think back to Chapter 1. Identify three things that you have learnt from reading this chapter. How will you consider these in relation to your own practice? What do you need to find out more about? Jot these down and think about them as we move to examine some practical strategies within Chapter 2.

2 The Learning Environment in a Neurodivergent World

Chapter Aims

- To consider the learning environment for neurodivergent pupils in your classroom.
- To think about the classroom layout and how this impacts your neurodivergent pupils.
- To begin to understand the complexities of the classroom environment for your neurodivergent pupils.
- To consider the communal spaces around schools and how they have an impact on your neurodivergent pupils.
- To begin to understand the sensory challenges and needs of your neurodivergent pupils within the school environment and the impact that this has on them.

Links to the Professional Standards for Teaching Assistants

Personal and Professional Conduct

- **5 Committing to improve their own** practice through self-evaluation and awareness.

Knowledge and Understanding

- **1 Acquire the appropriate skills, qualifications and/or experience** required for the teaching assistant role with support from the school employer.
- **2 Demonstrate expertise and skills in understanding the needs of all pupils** (including specialist expertise as appropriate) and know how to adapt and deliver support to meet individual needs.
- **3 Share responsibility for ensuring that their own knowledge and understanding is relevant and up to date** by reflecting on their

DOI: 10.4324/9781003427599-3

own practice, liaising with school leaders and accessing relevant professional development to improve personal effectiveness.

Teaching and Learning

- 1 Demonstrate an informed and efficient approach to teaching and learning by adopting relevant strategies to support the work of the teacher and increase achievement of all pupils including, where appropriate, those with special educational needs and disabilities.
- 5 Communicate effectively and sensitively with pupils to adapt to their needs and support their learning.
- 6 Maintain a stimulating and safe learning environment by organising and managing physical teaching space and resources.

Introduction

How are you feeling about implementing a neurodiverse model in your classroom? Have other practitioners within your school been discussing a neurodiversity model, or is it a new concept and language? What does your class teacher(s) know about neurodiversity? Is it a term that they use?

As we move into the content of the remaining chapters, it is important to acknowledge that as a member of support staff, you may have restrictions within your role and within your school. It is important to discuss new strategies and approaches with your class teacher, line manager or Special Educational Needs Co-ordinator (SENCo), but you may not be able to try out all of these strategies or approaches that you would like to. However, work with your colleagues to explore them and to improve your own practice.

Have you worked in a different school before? If so, how was this different in regard to the school ethos and principles? Their teaching methods, behaviour management strategies and policy and how they assess pupils may have been different. Each school is unique, and you will have to work within the framework of your own school ethos and policy, so ensure that you check with your colleagues before implementing something new.

If possible, discuss with other support staff from other schools their approaches to each of the chapter areas covered in this book, and you will see the range of perspectives you will gain from different schools.

The Classroom Environment for a Range of Different Pupils

Neurodivergence covers a huge range of differences as you have read in Chapter 1. Each of these will have an impact on the classroom and how pupils respond, react and behave. We, as educators, need to consider the barriers to learning that our neurodivergent pupils have and to reduce the negative impact that these barriers may have on pupils' outcomes. We can do this through developing an understanding of the neuro-differences that pupils have and the impact that this may have on the pupils when working in a class-room environment.

Many strategies that are discussed both within this chapter and within the other remaining chapters across the book are general strategies that could be used with and applied to all pupils regardless of their neuro-difference; other strategies are neuro-specific to pupils' neurodivergence.

Reflect

The first thing we need to consider is that the classroom is a very busy place. Think about this now: if you were an observer sitting at the back of the classroom and drawing upon all of your senses, what would you see, hear, smell and touch that would demonstrate this? At the busiest time of the day, what does your classroom look like, sound like and smell like?! Keep this in mind when we work through the chapter.

The SEN Register, Individual Education Plan and Education, Health and Care Plan

The impact of a busy classroom environment may be more challenging for neurodivergent pupils. We, as educational staff, need to consider what we can do to support our neurodivergent pupils and reduce the effect of this on pupil learning and progress.

Some neurodivergent pupils may be on the SEN register, and some won't, and this will depend specifically upon their area of need and the support that they may need to make progress. The SEN register is a register that the school is required to keep and that identifies the pupils who have additional needs that require further support and monitoring which are beyond what is normally expected for most pupils.

Pupils that are on this SEN register may also have an Individual Education Plan (IEP) which outlines the additional support or interventions that are needed. It will contain targets for the pupil, the supporting strategies that will be used to help the pupil make progress and achieve the targets and then a review of the impact of the targets. The IEP is reviewed at regular intervals and varies from school to school when this will be, but it is normally termly. The review is carried out between the SENCo, the parents or carers, and the pupil will have some input, either in the form of a discussion at the meeting or something recorded on paper before the meeting that will be presented. Depending upon the Local Authority (LA) the IEP may be known by a different name such as a 'One-Plan'.

Your class teacher will monitor the targets on the IEP, and it is likely that you, as a member of support staff, will be working directly with a child on an

IEP and will need to discuss with your class teacher how the pupil is progressing, for example, how they achieved towards learning objectives in a lesson when you have been working with them individually or within a group.

Some pupils with a higher level of need will have an Education, Health and Care Plan (EHCP). This plan identifies in great detail the challenges that the pupil faces and the support that is needed for the pupil to help them to progress. The LA allocates money via a banding process to the pupil with the EHCP, which, in most cases, is allocated to the school and will be used to support the facilitation of the plan. The EHCP is reviewed across the year, with a larger formal review which may be a multi-agency meeting at the end of the year, when the targets are reviewed and updated. Regular meetings and reviews ensure that the pupil is making progress towards their targets, or that the targets are reviewed and amended accordingly to any changes that are needed. Further reading on IEPs and EHCPs can be found in the 'Further Reading' section at the end of this chapter.

Using Classroom Space Effectively

We need to first consider the classroom space itself.

Activity

Think about one of your classrooms now, and sketch out what this looks like. Include:

- Table layouts
- Where resources are placed and access to them
- Displays – where are they and what is on them
- Seating arrangements for individual pupils

Make a note of whether table layouts are in groups, and if so, how many pupils are in the group around the table? Or do the pupils sit in rows? Or in tables of two? Which pupils sit where? Can the pupils all see the board without twisting in their seats? Can they see the teacher easily? Where are pupils sitting in relation to getting to the resources that they might need?

Professional Discussion

Discuss with your class teacher the layout of their classroom. Find out why they chose this layout. Did they consider research into different styles of layout? Is there a particular layout style for the school, department or year group? How did they decide which pupils would sit where? Were the different needs of the pupils accounted for, and were there any challenges in meeting the needs of all the pupils in this class? Has your teacher tried other classroom layouts before; if so, what was successful and what wasn't and why?

When considering the classroom layout and your neurodivergent pupils, there are several things that you will specifically need to consider:

- Neurodivergent pupils may need to be seated closer to an adult for reassurance or to access support.
- A buddy system may work well with particular pupils in which they can draw upon support and guidance from their peers.
- Some pupils may need to access natural daylight or fresh air throughout the day and be seated near a window (see the sensory considerations section for further information on this). Or they may prefer the opposite and prefer a darker, more dimly lit area of the room.
- Ensure that the tables and chairs are the correct heights for your pupils to avoid sensory discomfort. Do you need to add a cushion or footrest?
- Go back to your plan of your classroom that you drew, and consider where the resources are located. Where are the resources that are most commonly used stored? Where are pupils' trays located? Think about when a pupil needs to collect an item from their tray or a water bottle from the sink: who do they need to walk past, and are the gaps large enough so that pupils don't get bumped about? Your neurodivergent pupils may be best seated away from this area where they are less distracted, or there are less sensory issues of potentially being touched.
- Consider whether stationery items can be placed nearer pupils in a basket or tray to avoid lots of movement of other pupils near them. Neurodivergent pupils could be distracted or become upset or aggressive and want to remove themselves from the situation.

Displays

The use of displays is an important aspect of teaching and learning in the classroom. As a member of the support staff team, it might be your responsibility to put up the classroom displays or to organise the content. Your class teacher may have a particular ethos on the type of display that they want to have in their classroom or the purpose of different displays. There are some interesting articles to read on the place and purpose of displays in the 'Further Reading' section at the end of this chapter. Your school may have a policy on displays, and it is important that you read this and work within their policy. Discuss the use of displays with your class teacher: do they have a particular view on how they use their displays? For example, some schools will insist on plain, neutral background colours with little content on the boards. This is based upon studies including those by Hanley et al. (2017). Hanley et al. believe that the use of busy displays directly where pupils are learning can be distracting and hinder a child's progress, and this may be heightened for your neurodivergent pupils. In other schools you may see the opposite, with brightly coloured displays, tissue paper and hanging galas spilling out into the corridors. The purpose may be to create an atmosphere and engage pupils in creative writing through presenting visual scenes and settings from the current focus book or to engage pupils in the current theme, with some displays celebrating work and progress. Other displays might have a functional purpose: does your classroom have a working wall in which the teacher adds to across the week or topic with useful reminders for the pupils or formulae or processes to follow to support them to achieve the learning outcomes? This might include key vocabulary or methods to work out a maths problem. There are links to further reading on this area at the end of the chapter.

Professional Discussion

Discuss with your class teacher the type of displays that they use in their classroom and why. Is there a consistent approach across the school or is it up to the individual teacher as to what and how they use their display boards? Does your school have a policy on the use of displays?

Now that you have considered the use of displays in your own classrooms and school, we can apply what we know to what we are beginning to understand about our neurodivergent pupils.

Each neurodivergent pupil may react to display boards differently, so there is no one way or approach, and you may need to explore with your pupils what works for them or what might be distracting for them. For example, neurodivergent pupils may be supported to access the content on displays in a working wall. This may help by developing independence in progressing in tasks. For some pupils, a busy display may support developing creative ideas for story writing, but for others, it might prove distracting.

Consider where your neurodivergent pupils sit: are they near or facing displays that could potentially be useful for them or distracting? Some displays may be so busy that they become overwhelming, and pupils may not be able to select the information that they need to pull out from them.

Lessons with Movement

Many lessons contain elements of physical movement. Whether this is in and around the classroom, or outside in other areas of the school, they can pose challenges for neurodivergent pupils and they may have different expectations. Lessons such as Physical Education (PE), Science, Music, Art and

Design and Technology (D&T) will all have times in which pupils need to move out of their seats and navigate the space and other pupils to carry out their learning.

Whether you are support staff in a primary or secondary school, or attached to one class or several, at some point, your pupils will be taken out of their comfort zone, and their routines will become disrupted through movement in lessons.

So how do you tackle these challenges and support your neurodivergent pupils?

- Some neurodivergent pupils may have difficulty working with others or prefer to work alone rather than in pairs or groups. Think about the task that is being given: what are the learning outcomes to be met? Can your pupils carry this out on their own rather than with others and thus reduce anxiety, stress and conflict? Or do you need them to be working with others and will need to facilitate working together more closely and thoughtfully?
- Preparation: this is key when working with your neurodivergent pupils. Communicate prior to the lesson to prepare pupils and give them time to process the information on what it will look like. Talk through the structure of what the lesson will be and the expectations at each of the parts of the lesson. Use visual aids and reminders where needed. Try and incorporate a structure or routine that the pupil is already familiar with or will become familiar with over time and associate with that subject lesson.
- The use of more specialist equipment can be daunting and cause confusion for your neurodivergent pupils. Is there the opportunity to show pupils the equipment before the lesson? Or for pupils to handle and try the equipment before using and applying it within a formal lesson? Make time for pupils to develop their confidence in handling specialist equipment.
- Think about the relationships that your neurodivergent pupils have with their peers. When working with others, are they paired up with pupils that will be supportive? Will peers model desired behaviours to help overcome challenges? Further discussions on relationships between pupils will be explored further in Chapter 3.
- PE will bring specific additional challenges. PE will bring specific additional challenges; the movement within the lessons, the movement around the building, and the task of getting changed. Consider where your neurodivergent pupils will change. Changing rooms can be noisy, echo, and feel a little chaotic. Is there the option for neurodivergent pupils to change in a quieter, calmer space? The process of getting changed may feel rushed: can additional time be given? There may be issues with clothing, sensitivity to PE wear or difficulty with zips and buttons. Consider whether easier clothing to change in and out of, such as pull on jumpers or trousers with elastic, or clothing that can be worn throughout the day to avoid the changing and transisiton between lessons more smoothly.

Case Study

Susan is an LSA in a year 4 class. She supports Milo in particular throughout the majority of the day, but she also steps back to develop his independence and works with groups within the class. Milo has a diagnosis of attention-deficit hyperactivity disorder (ADHD). Susan was finding it increasingly difficult to support Milo during transitions between the lessons. Milo would become agitated and upset.

Recently the class teacher had changed pupil groupings after the recent assessment period, and Susan suspected that this may have had an impact due to the change and unfamiliarity of the pupils he was now working with and the places in which he was sitting in. Some of the behaviours that Milo was expressing were moving around the classroom at times when he should have been in his seat, refusing to stay in his seat, fidgeting, distracting other pupils and seeing if they would join in and delaying the start of the lesson.

What could be done to assess what is happening for Milo?

- First, consider what Milo's needs are, go back to the IEP or EHCP (if he has one) and see if there are any specific targets or strategies within this that would be useful to consider, apply or review.
- Take the time to observe what is happening. Observing thoroughly can enable you to gain a full picture. Sometimes it can be daunting to step back as we have a desire to step in and be 'doing something'. Look at the finer details: who is Milo needing to pass to get to his new seating positions? Does he need to collect equipment? Where is this? What other pupils are moving at the same time?
- Speak with Milo and ask him: what is happening for him for that is different? How does this feel? Did they prefer sitting in their previous places? Why?
- Consider the sensory elements that may be affecting Milo (further details later in this chapter). For example, note the lighting and air flow.

Once you have gathered all of this information, you will be able to start to unpick what is going on for Milo. Susan gathered this information and then sat with her class teacher to discuss what she had observed and the information she had received from Milo.

They discussed the possible ways forward and the implications for each:

- Keep Milo where he was, and move some of the other groups for less distraction. This might be fine for Milo, but it may have a knock-on effect for other neurodivergent pupils in the class.

- Make some adjustments to the positions of the tables so that Milo had less movement around the classroom.
- Provide some time in between the transitions for Milo to get a sensory break (as outlined later in the chapter) before resettling back to work. Although this might mean that there is a delay for Milo, it is better to have a focused start to the lesson.
- Provide Milo with his own tray of resources linked to each lesson already laid out on his table.
- Discuss with Milo in advance any table or grouping changes to better prepare him.

Susan and the class teacher worked together to implement some of these changes which included moving Milo onto a table that was nearer to the teacher, and ensuring that there was plenty of space around Milo's chair so that he wasn't being bumped by his peers moving to their positions, and that his resources where prepared in advance and ready for him on his table. Once Milo settled in to his new routine and had less distractions; the transitions became smoother and the start of the lesson became quicker. Going through this process supported Susan to develop her skills in unpicking the issues and then implementing and reviewing the changes.

Case Study

Marvin is a TA in a Physical Education (PE) class within a secondary school. He specialises in pastoral support for pupils and enjoys developing positive relationships with them. Marvin is struggling with the challenges of one of his pupils: Jack who is in year 10. Jack has a diagnosis of autism spectrum condition and anxiety. Jack arrives late for PE or doesn't turn up at all. This starts happening after the return to the classroom after COVID. Marvin noticed that when Jack engaged in PE, he seemed to enjoy the lessons taking an active part in them. He was skilled in areas such as football and rugby, and he enjoyed using the gym. However, as the last year passed, he engaged less and failed to turn up to classes often.

   Marvin arranged to meet with the class teacher and the SENCo and discuss his concerns with them and seek some support from them to try and engage Jack further.

Firstly, they unpicked the possible reasons for Jack's disengagement:

- The initial enthusiasm for the return to school after COVID had worn off.
- Changes in the curriculum topics may not appeal to Jack.
- Pupils had moved from arriving at school in their PE kit on PE days and staying in kit all day to pre-COVID routines of bringing in kit and changing for PE.

Marvin then arranged to meet with Jack and discuss with him how he was feeling about PE and see if they could make some adjustments for him.

Jack stated that he really enjoyed the lesson itself (just as Marvin had identified), but it was everything that surrounded the lesson that caused Jack anxiety and led to him not wanting to attend.

Together, Marvin and Jack noted that the following areas seemed to cause Jack some difficulty:

- The changing rooms were busy even when staff were in there, and the other boys could become boisterous.
- The noise levels in the changing rooms were very loud and echoed which Jack didn't like.
- Changing for PE was rushed; Jack would become anxious that he couldn't change in time for the lesson or might be late for his following lesson, so he worried about it and preferred not to attend to avoid being told off for being late.

Marvin (with support from the teacher and SENCo) put in the following strategies to support Jack:

- The quiet staff changing room was opened for Jack to change in alone.
- Jack was given clear directions on how to locate the staff changing room, and then how to move from there to the field or sports hall.
- Jack was given reassurance that his teachers knew that it was ok if Jack was a little late following a PE lesson.
- Jack set an alarm on his watch for five minutes before the end of the PE lesson, so that he could leave earlier to get changed.

The impact of these strategies meant that:

- The changing area was quiet for Jack.
- Jack knew how to get to the areas he needed to.
- Jack's anxiety was reduced and he felt reassured.

These adjustments were then added to Jack's IEP.

Outside the Classroom Space

Adjustments may need to be made outside the classroom in the wider school environment too. There are many spaces within the school that could prove challenging to your neurodivergent pupils. These places include corridors, assembly, break times, lunch times, canteen areas and small working spaces for interventions. We will now look at each of these in turn.

Corridors

Corridors can be one of the most challenging spaces for a neurodivergent pupil in school. In both primary and secondary schools, corridors are scary places full of noise and bustling pupils. There is often very little natural light or air flow; they may contain lots of notices and distractions and, to a neurodivergent pupil, may hold lots of threats and anxieties.

You will need to consider carefully how this space is managed, and as a member of support staff, it may be your role to ensure that your neurodivergent pupils get from one place to another without any disturbances.

Think about:

- Can your pupils move around the corridors at a quieter time of the day? Is their provision in your school for a child to leave the classroom five minutes earlier and make their way to another class before the corridors become full?
- Can your pupils vocalise their journey so you can ensure that they know where they are going and how to get there?
- Does the pupil need an adult to escort them during these times or to have a buddy system in place with a peer to escort them, particularly when timetables are new or it is for something unfamiliar?

When considering the nature and purpose of the journey around the school, look out for:

- Is the signposting clear? Can your pupils understand and follow the signposting, or do they need additional support such as practicing their route?
- Are corridors kept tidy and clear without distraction?

Assemblies

Assemblies can be a key cause in anxiety for some neurodivergent pupils, particularly your autistic pupils. Think about the structure and content of an assembly, large numbers of pupils and staff gathered, being stuck in the middle of a large number of people and not being able to leave, echoing noise, bright lighting and noise from videos, music or screens being used.

Reflect

Reflect on the needs of one of your neurodivergent pupils within an assembly and possible strategies that you could implement and try out.

- Can your pupil give you a signal indicating that they are becoming anxious and need to leave? Practice this with them so that they feel reassured.
- Can your pupil be placed at the end of a line so that if they need to leave they have permission to take themselves out?
- Can you discuss with your pupil the content of the assembly and prepare them for any noisy resources or equipment of videos that may be used?
- Consider whether your pupil *needs* to go to the assembly: could information be given to them in a different format?

It may vary from assembly to assembly depending on the content and focus, resources being used and how your pupil is already feeling that day.

Break and Lunch Times

Break and lunch times can be a challenging time of the day for some of your neurodivergent pupils. We know that large spaces with lots of people may cause anxiety or disorientation, echo and be noisy. On top of this, the lack of routine and choices to be made, such as where to sit and who to sit with, could change on a daily basis. The smell of different foods daily could cause some issues for your neurodivergent pupils with sensory challenges; combined with all of these other factors, pupils may become overstimulated.

Consider what strategies may be useful for your neurodivergent pupils during these times.

- Is it possible for pupils to move to a smaller, quieter area to eat lunch or to have a break?
- Are there structured activities set up in areas of the school that your pupils could attend? Maybe are there facilitated games or crafts? How do pupils

access them? Can pupils find the activities easily if they would like to take themselves there? If not, can activities such as these be set up?
- Are there the facilities for quieter, calmer areas located throughout the school, safe spaces where your pupils can go?
- Is there a buddy system in place where another pupil can check in with your neurodivergent pupils and help them find places to go to if needed?

Sensory Considerations

Neurodivergent pupils with sensory issues can face additional challenges in the school environment. As we have seen in Chapter 1, sensory processing disorder (SPD) can co-occur with other neurodivergencies such as autism and ADHD or be a condition in itself.

This Case Study explores a pupil with SPD and the impact on them and considerations that need to be made.

Case Study

Ravi was a pupil in year 6 in a mainstream primary school. He was due to transition to secondary school, and his parents were worried about how he would cope with this. Ravi was autistic and had a diagnosis of ADHD and general anxiety disorder. His attendance at school was poor. Over the past two years, it had deteriorated to a level of just 35% attendance on an average week. The SENCo was seeking further support from outside agencies to see if they could increase his attendance and prepare him for transition.

The main issue appeared to be that Ravi had difficulty coming in to school, breaking away from his mum and physically getting him on to site. He would arrive for school, become very distressed and return home with his mum. On the days that he managed to come onto the school site and in to his classroom, he seemed to settle in reasonably well to school life and routines and enjoy mixing with his peers and the learning taking place.

The first assessment needed was to identify the barriers to Ravi coming onto the school site. Was this related to attachment issues and not wanting to leave his mum, his anxiety in leaving her or additional issues that hadn't yet been identified?

The SENCo decided to step back and carry out some observations for several days running to try and gain a full picture of what seemed to be happening.

It was noted that mum would come into reception with Ravi, where a handover to Ravi's TA was attempted to be made. There was reassurance, distraction and encouragement tried, but it often led to escalation and mum following Ravi as he headed off back down the school lane and home again.

During these observations, the SENCo noticed Ravi wiping his nose and covering it, screwing up his face and becoming increasingly agitated. On day three, when this happened, the SENCo intervened; she took Ravi outside and asked him: what was going on for him? Ravi stated he hated the smell of the building; it was overpowering and filled his thoughts. It was an old musty building that the reception area was located in, and the musty smell lingered in the entrance. Ravi stated he just wanted to go home where his house smelled nicer and he could smell his dog and the cooking.

It is something that hadn't occurred to the professionals as they themselves hadn't realised this was potentially a big issue for Ravi. They had noticed the smell, but as neurotypical people, they had dismissed it as they did every day that they entered the building.

The TA (with support from the SENCo) carried out a sensory walk with Ravi and his mum around the school. She noted down how Ravi felt in different parts of the building and what he could see, hear and smell to give them a broader picture of his sensory needs.

They agreed with Ravi that he should enter the building each day through the side entrance to his classroom instead, which was located in the new part of the building. This increased Ravi's attendance to 75% almost immediately.

By taking account of Ravi's hypersensitivity to smells, improvements were made for Ravi to access his learning. A sensory walk was also carried out at his new school with the TA who was supporting Ravi in his transition to secondary school.

The recognition of the impact of SPD is really important, as noted in the above case study with Ravi. SPD can have a significant impact on learning and access to it. As discussed in Chapter 1, SPD includes both hyper- and hyposensitivity in the areas of smell, taste, touch, hearing, vision, movement, body position and gravity. Recognising how SPD affects an individual and putting in strategies to support or counteract hyper- or hyposensitivity can be beneficial throughout the day. The next sections will look at each area in turn, the possible impact, and the strategies that could be considered for each area.

Smell

As seen with Ravi, pupils may be hypersensitive to different smells. This could include perfumes or aftershaves, cooking smells and smells of a building or furniture. As with Ravi, someone with SPD may have more intense reactions to certain smells than that of a neurotypical person, and they may have stronger reactions such as becoming distracted or irritable by them. Other pupils with SPD may want to seek out smells instead and demonstrate behaviours such as sniffing clothes to seek the scent of the detergent, the smell of the materials such as plastic toys, or be tempted to put things up their noses.

Things to consider:

- If you wear a strong scent, consider changing this for something more neutral or lighter if you think it is a trigger for a pupil with SPD.
- If you are working with pupils closely, think about what you may have had to eat or drink at break or lunch time – no one likes coffee breath when they are trying to learn!
- Set up scent-seeking activities for younger pupils to gain sensory-seeking input.

Taste

Many pupils with SPD may have sensitivity to tastes and textures. This may limit food choices, and they may prefer to eat the same safe foods over and over again. They may not like food being mixed on the same plate, or they may seek out tastes and want to lick objects.

Things to consider:

- Set up tasting sessions to introduce new foods, tastes and textures.
- Make sure there are safe foods available at lunch time and break times; this may need to be food from home.
- Chewy toys can help with the sensory aspects inside the mouth and are often useful for supporting younger pupils.

Touch

Again, pupils may be hyper- or hyposensitive to touch. Some pupils may not like or want to be touched and physically shy away from contact, even with the slightest of touches such as someone brushing past them. Other pupils, or even the same pupils but at different times, may want to seek out touch and want to be hugged very tightly.

Things to consider:

- Use a no-pressure approach. Do not make a child hold hands if they do not want to or play games that include physical touch as this may feel very uncomfortable for the child to the point of hypersensitivity giving the feeling of pain.
- Introduce experiences where touch may be needed slowly, but remember, we should not be enforcing this on a child, just because it is seen as normal in a neurotypical world.
- Pressure toys can be a useful way to support the need for hugs without physical contact from a member of staff. For example, weighted blankets

can be easily included within primary classrooms or the use of heavy rucksacks for secondary aged pupils. Some of these have additional straps to create tightness across the back and chest for a sensory-seeking teenager.

Sound

This can be a difficult sense in the classroom. There are many distractions caused by sound that neurotypical people can block out, but for neurodivergent pupils they can become a distraction.
Things to consider:

- Small sounds such as a tap dripping or clock ticking can be distracting for you neurodivergent pupil. They may find it extremely difficult to block this out.
- Conversations from groups of other peers can be incredibly distracting, with your neurodivergent pupil focusing on conversations that are not their own.
- Consider noise levels within the classroom and where your pupils are sitting: can they sit with no groups behind them so they can focus on the conversation directly in front of them?
- Can your pupil use noise-cancelling headphones to block out unwanted sounds when they are working on a piece of work? There are small in ear headphones for you older pupils that are more discreet.
- Pupils may become incredibly distressed by loud sudden noises such as a fire alarm, hand dryers in the toilets or items being dropped. Pupils may need linger to regulate after there has been an incident such as this.

Vision

Some pupils may prefer artificial light of varying strengths; others may prefer the use of natural light. Pupils may hold objects close to their face to filter out any distractions, or they may like to watch spinning toys or flashing lights.
Things to consider:

- Is there the availability of a sensory room, and can sensory breaks be incorporated within the day to this room?
- Where is your pupil located in the classroom, what sensory input are they getting and do they need something different?
- When pupils begin to tire, they may need something else and may need some sensory stimulation instead, needing a change of focus or task.

Movement

Pupils may seek sensory activities such as spinning, climbing or rocking. Creating a movement such as this is known as stimming. You should not prevent a child from stimming if they are not harming themselves or anyone else.

Things to consider:

- Give opportunities throughout the day for pupils to encounter movement such as access to a climbing frame, swing, or through the use of fidget toys.

Body Position

Some pupils with SPD may have an unusual walking gait or movement. They may want to sit in a position that is not seen as being appropriate to sit in on a chair to write or on the carpet during focused input time. It could include slouching or tucking their legs underneath them.

Things to consider:

- Is the chair appropriate for them, and can they make themselves comfortable?

Gravity

Gravitational insecurity can affect balance and the ability to process vestibular stimulation in pupils with SPD. This can cause your pupil to avoid activities such as the use of an escalator, lift, fair ground rides or heights. This could have an impact on the child's involvement in school trips. In school, they could be fearful of PE, being upside down or using climbing equipment.

Thing to consider:

- Include sensory breaks throughout the day, and build up vestibular activities slowly.

Chapter Summary

This chapter has asked you to reflect upon classroom layout and consider further the implications of this for your neurodivergent pupils. By taking a step back and observing, you can gain information that you may have not seen before. Consider the choices made in table layouts, access to resources and the use of displays, and how these affect your different neurodivergent learners. Communal spaces in schools can be problematic and overstimulating for your pupils. They may need planning for with additional support for unstructured times. Finally, there was an overview of the areas of sensory need, considering the impact of hyper- and hyposensitivity.

Chapter 3 will be looking at behaviour management for neurodivergent pupils. Begin to think about particular pupils you work with and the strategies you are using: are they effective, what works and what doesn't? Make some notes which will be useful as we move into Chapter 3.

Glossary of Key Terms

- Educational, Health and Care Plan (EHCP) – a plan based on an assessment by the Local Authority to identify and support the needs of individual pupils.
- Individual Education Plan (IEP) – a school support plan for a pupil with identified additional needs.
- Local Authority (LA) – the local administrative body in local government responsible for the public services and facilities in a local area.
- Pedagogy – the method and practice of teaching. It could include teaching methods, feedback and assessment.

Further Reading

IEPs and EHCPS

Education Advocacy. What Is an EHCP? https://educationadvocacy.co.uk/what-is-a-ehcp/.

Gov.uk. Children with Special Educational Needs and Disabilities (SEND). www.gov.uk/children-with-special-educational-needs/extra-SEN-help.

IPSEA. Educational, Health and Care Plans. www.ipsea.org.uk/pages/category/education-health-and-care-plans.

Special Educational Needs Advice Centre (SENAC). What Is an Individual Education Plan (IEP). https://senac.co.uk/advice/what-is-an-iep-individual-education-plan/#:~:text=Individual%20Education%20Plans%20are%20written,your%20child%20to%20focus%20on.

Classroom Displays

Diminque, R. (2021) Creating an Effective Classroom Display, What Does the Research Say? www.teachermagazine.com/sea_en/articles/creating-an-effective-classroom-display-what-does-the-research-say Teacher Magazine.

Nguyen, B. (2021) Minimising Classroom Displays. https://teachthinkblog.wordpress.com/2021/04/06/minimising-classroom-displays/.

Teach, Think Blog.

Willingham, D. (2014) Are Decorated Classroom Walls Too Distracting? www.danielwillingham.com/daniel-willingham-science-and-education-blog/are-decorated-classroom-walls-too-distracting.

Classroom Organisation

National Autistic Society (2018) Neurodiversity in Education. www.autism.org.uk/advice-and-guidance/professional-practice/neurodiversity-education.

Social Stories

Gray, C. (2015). *The New Social Story Book*. Future Horizons, Arlington.
Timmins, S. (2017). *Successful Social Stories for School and College Students with Autism*. Jessica Kingsley Publishers, London.

Reference

Hanley, M., Khairat, M., Taylor, K., Wilson, R., Cole-Fletcher, R. and Riby, D. (2017) Classroom Displays - Attraction Or Distraction? Evidence of Impact on Attention and Learning from Children with and without Autism. *Developmental Psychology*. Vol. 53. No. 7. P1265–75.

Reflect

Looking back at Chapter 2, are there any elements of the classroom layout that could be impacting upon your neurodivergent pupils? Is there something that you would like to discuss with your class teacher that might support any of your pupils?

You have started to consider neurodivergent pupils' sensory needs: are you looking at the classroom environment differently now? If so, how?

Chapter 3 will examine behaviour management in relation to your neurodivergent pupils, and you will see that there are overlapping elements to classroom layout, sensory needs and behaviour.

3 Behaviour Management and Neurodivergent Pupils

Chapter Aims

- To understand the behavioural challenges faced by support staff, and to begin to identify the underlying causes for this with neurodivergent pupils.
- To develop relationships with neurodivergent pupils and their parent and carers.
- To begin to implement and try out a range of strategies to support neurodivergent pupils in your classes.
- To begin to develop and use positive language and communication to support behaviour management with your neurodivergent pupils.
- To understand the behaviour models used in schools and how the behaviour policy is followed.

Links to the Professional Standards for Teaching Assistants

Personal and Professional Conduct

- **1 Having personal and professional regard for the ethos, policies and practices of the school** in which they work as professional members of staff.
- **2 Demonstrating positive attitudes, values and behaviours** to develop and sustain effective relationships with the school community.
- **5 Committing to improve their own practice** through self-evaluation and awareness.

Knowledge and Understanding

- **1 Acquire the appropriate skills, qualifications and/or experience** required for the teaching assistant role with support from the school employer.

DOI: 10.4324/9781003427599-4

- **2 Demonstrate expertise and skills in understanding the needs of all pupils** (including specialist expertise as appropriate) and know how to adapt and deliver support to meet individual needs.
- **3 Share responsibility for ensuring that their own knowledge and understanding is relevant and up to date** by reflecting on their own practice, liaising with school leaders and accessing relevant professional development to improve personal effectiveness.
- **5 Understand their roles and responsibilities within the classroom and whole school context** recognising that these may extend beyond a direct support role.

Teaching and Learning

- 1 Demonstrate an informed and efficient approach to teaching and learning adopting relevant strategies to support the work of the teacher and increase achievement of all pupils including, where appropriate, those with special educational needs and disabilities (SEND).
- 3 Use effective behaviour management strategies consistently in line with the school's policy and procedures.
- 5 Communicate effectively and sensitively with pupils to adapt to their needs and support their learning.

Working with Others

- **1 Recognise and respect the role and contribution of other professionals, parents and carers** by liaising effectively and working in partnership with them.
- **4 Understand their role** in order to be able to work collaboratively with classroom teachers and other colleagues, including specialist advisory teachers.

Introduction

Developing an understanding of the underlying causes of challenging behaviour is really interesting, and although at times this can be challenging, work with your neurodivergent pupils to gain insight into what is behind the behaviour, and to find strategies to move unwanted behaviour into a more positive and workable approach is crucial. Sometimes you will see the impact of strategies straight away, and others may take some time, so don't be disheartened or frustrated; continue working with your pupils and enjoy the challenges and new learning knowledge and skills for yourself that this brings.

You may have been on training courses around behaviour or been given some induction within your school; for others this may be limited. This chapter will begin to unpick some of the challenges that you will face and give you ideas that you may want to research more on or seek further training on.

There are many layers to successful behaviour management; there are basic strategies that work for most pupils, most of the time, and you will need to work at developing and building relationships with pupils – which can take some considerable time. You will need to develop consistency in using strategies between school and home, and it may be your role to communicate this.

What Does Behaviour Look Like in the Classroom? What Are the Contributing Factors That Underlie This Behaviour?

Although it can be frustrating listening to pupils chattering while you are talking or not responding when you direct them to stop, these sorts of low-level behaviours for the majority of your class can normally be addressed through applying your school's behaviour policy. Observe strategies that your class teacher uses and what works effectively for them, and follow their lead as this will ensure consistency and pupils normally like the routine and familiarity of the strategies.

When considering more challenging types of behaviour in class, there are often underlying reasons and causes that are driving this behaviour. Challenging behaviours could take the form of pupils finding it difficult to settle into work, refusing to carry out tasks, walking around the classroom and disrupting the flow of the lesson or other pupils, leaving the classroom, shouting or calling out, swearing or using inappropriate language, damaging the classroom or equipment and, in extreme cases, violent behaviour towards their peers or members of staff.

As a member of support staff, you may be required to work with a neurodivergent pupil that is exhibiting this type of behaviour, and you may need to seek more specialist training and support from experienced members of staff and guidance from an Education, Health and Care Plan (EHCP) or Individual Education Plan (IEP). Never feel afraid to ask for further help and guidance; this will develop your knowledge and skills and should be viewed positively.

The next sections of this chapter will give an overview of the elements that could be impacting on a pupil's behaviour. These elements could be in isolation, or it could be a complex mix of elements.

Anxiety

Anxiety will be discussed in further detail in Chapter 4 as part of pupil wellbeing. As an overview, it is important to recognise that pupil behaviour can be affected by anxiety. Anxiety can be detrimental to a pupil's behaviour in that they may want to avoid certain situations which could lead to a pupil leaving the classroom, refusing to come in or expressing anger.

There are many other neuro-differences such as autism spectrum condition and attention-deficit hyperactivity disorder (ADHD) that co-occur with anxiety, and therefore, it could have an effect on how anxiety presents and which areas of the spectrum are more challenging to a pupil.

Dysregulation

Dysregulation, also known as emotional dysregulation, is the inability to manage emotions and behaviours in a neurotypical way or range. Instead, emotions such as anger, irritability, frustration and sadness may become heightened and prominent in your pupils' daily life.

Dysregulation can show as erratic behaviour when emotions can become uncontrollable quickly and unexpectedly. Levels of adrenaline are increased and pupils can enter a fight or flight mode, which is inappropriate for a classroom environment. Remember, however, that this could be out of their control, and it is the body and brain's physical response to a situation. On the other hand, pupils may become the opposite and become withdrawn, forgetful or numb. This may be seen when you are asking them to do something but not gaining a response.

Some pupils may be more susceptible to dysregulation, and this would include those with attachment issues, foetal alcohol spectrum disorder, past trauma and social, emotional and mental health (SEMH).

Key behaviours that can be seen by dysregulated pupils are:

- Attention-seeking behaviours.
- Poor attitudes to work, including the refusal to start a task or walking away from tasks.
- The inability to cope with daily tasks and routines.

Oppositional Defiance Disorder

The challenging behaviour associated with oppositional defiance disorder (ODD) could present itself as the refusal to carry out tasks, work or follow instructions. There could be a lack of cooperation with peers and adults, and the pupil may appear to start arguments and to question authority such as the class and school rules.

Sensory Processing Disorder

As outlined in further detail in Chapter 2, sensory processing disorder (SPD) can cause unwanted and challenging behaviours such as a pupil leaving the classroom or getting away from the overstimulated sensory overloads that they are experiencing. Ensure that you observe what may be causing these hyper- or hyposensitivity experiences, and consider whether strategies to support your neurodivergent pupils can be implemented.

Developing Positive Relationships with Neurodivergent Pupils

Building positive relationships with your neurodivergent pupils is key to managing challenging behaviour and to developing your effectiveness of using supportive strategies to engage pupils. It is important to set boundaries in your working relationship with pupils as well as being a support for them and guiding them on managing their behaviour and emotions. Becoming too friendly with your pupils can be detrimental to the relationship that you build with them; your strategies may become ineffective as pupils push and cross the boundaries as they think of you as being a friend, so it is important to develop a sustainable working balance when developing and maintaining relationships with them.

There are many ways to develop your pupil/support staff professional relationship with pupils, which include:

- Start the day off by greeting pupils (and parents and carers if relevant) at the door and use pupil names.
- Ensure that you enable time in your day to get to know and understand your pupils, what are they like as individuals? What do they engage with out of school and what are their interests?
- Where possible, give your pupils responsibilities, and show them that you trust them to carry these out with care.
- Use praise when effort is used.
- Ensure that you are respectful to pupils at all times, even when you need to challenge or address unwanted behaviour.
- It is vital that you listen carefully to your pupil's pint of view when an incident has occurred. Pupils easily feel un-listened to or unheard when they are involved in a challenging situation with a peer.
- Give a pupil time to ensure that they feel understood.
- Key to building relationships is not to hold a grudge. As an adult, it is tempting to feel hurt by something a pupil has done or said and be assured; the pupil has not set out to hurt you. There are reasons for their behaviour. Repair the positive relationship as quickly as you can and move on from this.

The key element to remember in this chapter is that relationships are at the heart of good behaviour management, strategies can be learnt, but relationships take time to build.

Case Study

Marcus was a TA in a large secondary school. He had a pupil with a diagnosis of ODD and SEMH, who he was supporting across a range of classes and subjects. He was working on developing his relationship with

Leya, but he was he finding it challenging and frustrating as he couldn't see instant results.

Marcus decided to draw upon the experience of other colleagues, and he sent an email out to a few other experienced TAs, the Special Educational Needs Co-ordinator (SENCo) and some of the class teachers that taught Leya. He asked for some advice and specific strategies that might help him to build his relationship with Leya and be able to encourage her to participate in lessons further rather than the consistent refusal he was getting. He was worried that time was slipping by, and he was being ineffective in supporting her and moving her learning on.

Marcus received supportive emails in his responses. Experienced staff advised that Leya could be difficult in their classes too and he wasn't alone in this.

Some key feedback was included:

- Other TAs were experiencing the same thing in their classes that they supported.
- Where there were positive relationships and engagement, Marcus was advised that there was no 'quick fix', and it would take some time for the relationship to develop.
- Advice on 'showing that you care' was given.

Marcus felt reassured that he was not the only TA feeling this, and he started to take the pressure off himself. This, in turn, enabled him to be more relaxed around Leya and not apply as much pressure to her and enjoy the time he spent with her getting to know her, her interests and what would potentially engage her. She had low self-esteem, and tackling work often made her feel worse about herself.

Marcus then started to model and engage in the work himself: having a go, getting things wrong and verbally engaging Leya to support him so that they could do it together. He never applied pressure to engage Leya, and he let her engage as and when she wanted to. He progressed to starting something and then needing to leave temporarily to deal with something else, and Leya began to finish tasks by the time he had returned. He built a trusting relationship with Leya, and they began working together to build her self-esteem and engagement in lessons.

Marcus identified that although it took some considerable time to get to this point, he had begun to understand Leya, read her body language and consider how she was feeling; he knew when to give praise, encouragement or direction and when to walk away and give Leya space to process information.

General Strategies for Manging Behaviour and How They Impact Neurodivergent Pupils

Tom Bennet is a key behaviour management trainer and had worked with the Department for Education (DfE) on providing guidance for trainee teachers on managing behaviour basics in the classroom. His work is useful to read and draw upon, and there is a link in the 'Further Reading' section of this chapter to his behaviour toolkit.

Bennett focuses his work around three key areas:

- Proactive behaviour management: planning for behaviour management rather than just reacting to poor behaviour.
- Norms: understanding what your normal classroom looks like for you and how to move pupils back on track to this when they step outside the norms.
- Routines: using routines and embedding these into your classroom practice.

Some general strategies that you will be using, be observing others use, or learn to use will include:

- The use of class and school rules and routines.
- Using reward systems including individual rewards, class based and school based (e.g. house points).
- Using sanctions or consequences including using warnings and a choice.
- The use of praise and proximity praise including positive rule reminders.
- Ignoring unwanted behaviour intentionally.
- Using body language such as a stern look, shake of the head or crossing your arms.
- Using questioning to check whether a pupil understands what they need to be doing and why.
- Time to think things through.

Also consider learning behaviours or behaviour for learning. This outlines different types of behaviour that pupils need to be doing to be able to learn effectively. Ellis and Todd (2018) and Mould (2020) write on this key area of behaviour management and outline three areas in which pupils need to demonstrate the following behaviours: emotional – naming emotions, managing impulses and showing pride in success; social – focusing on learning, listening to the teacher and showing empathy; cognitive – having good organisation, setting goals and monitoring own progress and talking purposively with peers (Mould, 2020).

As we already know from Chapter 1, some of these learning behaviours could be incredibly difficult for neurodivergent pupils. Just taking one aspect such as organisation could prove very difficult for autistic or ADHD pupils.

The Education Endowment Foundation (EEF) conducts independent evidence-based research within education. It is a good source of advice, guidance and strategies across a range of educational subjects. The EEF (2019) developed a guidance report which included recommendations for improving behaviour in schools.

These included:

1 Know and understand your pupils (as we can see, this is important from the case study with Marcus and Leya).
2 Teach learning behaviours alongside managing unwanted behaviours.
3 Support good classroom behaviour.
4 Use simple approaches as part of your regular routines in class.
5 Use targeted approaches to meet the need of your individual pupils.
6 Ensure that you have whole school consistency.

So What Else Might Be Needed?

You may need to go a step further with your neurodivergent pupils that are outside general behaviour management guidance, strategies and advice. It is therefore important to assess pupil needs which will be carried out by your class teacher and SENCo, but they will certainly require your input if you are working with the pupil. This will follow the 'graduated approach' which is outlined in detail in Chapter 5.

Pupils may need to have sensory breaks planned into their day, rather than reacting to sensory overload when this happens, or need access to a learning or support hub within the school, or specialist resources and equipment.

Professional Discussion

Discuss with your class teacher which behaviour management strategies that they use in their daily practice that they believe are the most effective for them. Why is this effective? Do you think this is a strategy that works, or could work for you?

Are there particular strategies that you feel are more effective with your neurodivergent pupils? Or any areas in which you are having particular challenges and need further support with?

In the following section, consider the primary case study in which a TA needs further support with managing behaviour.

Case Study

Amara was allocated to working in one class which had a number of neurodivergent pupils in. She was new to her TA role and was struggling with managing the behaviour of one pupil, Ethan, that became dysregulated frequently. The pupil had an EHCP, a diagnosis of autism and SPD, and they had several strategies in place in the classroom. Amara was using a visual timetable to support Ethan, a personalised reward chart and some sensory toys, and gave him regular breaks. Ethan also accessed the lunch club which was facilitated by the learning mentor in the school and supported pupils in engaging with others in play.

However, even with this range of strategies in place, Amara was finding it difficult to manage Ethan's behaviour during lesson time. Ethan would become agitated and disengaged from activities frequently throughout the day, and Amara was beginning to feel that she had run out of options and strategies to draw upon.

Amara and her class teacher decided to speak with the SENCo and see what further support could be accessed within the school. The school had a nurture room in which a tepee sat within a cordoned off area. It was a dark, quiet space with cushions and other soft furnishings for pupils to access if they needed somewhere quiet to regulate. The SENCo suggested how they could incorporate this into their day, introducing to Ethan that this was a safe and quiet space if he needed to use it for short periods of time. Over the course of the next two weeks, Ethan was introduced to the space with Amara, and they sat and read or listened to music. Ethan then began to use the space when he became agitated and disengaged. He would access this to have some time to himself when feeling overwhelmed with the activities, busyness and noise level in the class. Amira began to see how the tepee corner was helping Ethan to regulate more quickly and be able to return to the classroom having had time away. This in turn increased his engagement when he was in the classroom.

Reflect

What additional whole school resources does your school have? Are these accessible for your neurodivergent pupils? Are there any in particular that could support behaviour management through the regulation of emotions of some of your pupils? How would you access them?

The Importance of Language

Within schools, staff and pupils communicate in a range of ways: verbal, written and visual. Difficulties relating to communication are prominent in the neurodiverse population which has implications for pupil learning and progress.

Reflect

What different types of communication can you recall in your setting? How do each of these cause challenges for your neurodivergent pupils?

The Challenges of Verbal Communication for Neurodivergent Pupils' section will focus on verbal communications, and written and visual forms of communications will be addressed in Chapter 6 looking at different teaching strategies.

The Challenges of Verbal Communication for Neurodivergent Pupils

The use of spoken language can be very complex, and when we consider that some of our neurodivergent pupils will have language processing difficulties, we need to consider how we talk with pupils more carefully to limit confusion and misunderstandings.

Reflect

Remember a time in the last week when you have given a pupil a set of instructions: did they understand your request? How do you know?

Activity

Take each of these statements, and consider what your neurodivergent pupils might find difficult about them and jot them down:

1 'Julie, it may have escaped your notice, but Zainab is not at the other end of the classroom!'
2 'Do you understand what you need to do?'
3 'Aleya, stop that please'
4 'Go on, hurry up, there is a seat in the corner'
5 'I've told you what to do, now get on and do it'
6 'Amir, why don't you ask if you don't understand?'

Have you noted down some of the following issues?

1 The sentence is not clear and has a lot of information in it. Julie may know that Zainab is not at the other end of the classroom, but not understand what you actually mean by it.

2 Often pupils will nod in agreement as they will want to get things right and to please you as the adult. However, they may not have actually understood what they need to do.

3 Stop what?

4 What is the instruction? They may know where the seat is, but not be sure about your expectations of them needing to sit in it.

5 You are assuming that they understand what they need to do.

6 Amir may think that they do understand what they need to do but might not understand.

So how could you change your language to be clearer and more direct, and check on the understanding of your neurodivergent learners? You will need to ensure that you are using clarity of language such as:

1 Be clear with the behaviour you are wanting. 'Julie, you will need to use your table voice for this activity, thank you'.

2 'Jack, can you repeat back to me what are the steps that you need to do to complete your work?'

3 'Aleya, you need to stop walking around the classroom now, and come and join us sitting on your chair here at your desk'.

4 'Ruan, there is an empty chair over in the corner next to the sink, please go and sit in that one, thanks'.

5 'Nadeem, what should you be doing? Can you tell me?'

6 Check frequently on your pupils: have they grasped what you have asked them to do, or do you need to reframe or re-explain in a different way?

There are some further ways that can support your pupils when using verbal language:

- Use the child's name at the beginning of any instruction or communication so that they are clear that you are speaking to them.
- Give clear instructions that are positively framed; tell them what you want them to be doing, not what you want them to stop. For example, 'Suki, walk in the corridor, thank you' rather than 'stop running!'.
- Use short sentences with one piece of information in it.
- Use 'thanks' at the end of a sentence rather than 'please' (when appropriate) as it shows that you expect compliance, rather than giving them a choice.

There are specific strategies that can be very useful for pupils with ODD; for example, Hook and Vass (2016) developed a strategy using 'maybe'…'and'…as part of a script. It is very effective and deflects conflict, bringing pupils back on task. I will summarise the strategy below, but have a look in further detail by going to the work of Hook and Vass which is in the 'Further Reading' section and references list at the end of the chapter.

I'll present a scenario where a pupil is doing something that they shouldn't, and you try and redirect them. They become agitated and defensive, saying that wasn't what they were doing and there is the potential for escalation. By using the following script, de-escalation and refocussing of the pupil back on task is applied:

Staff member: Lucas, you are not paying attention to the maths problem that I am explaining to you, and you have just handed Kai a note instead.

Lucas: I wasn't doing anything!! It's not fair, you always start on me. (The staff member saw Lucas handing over the note and might feel like challenging Lucas, but decides on the following option to handle the situation.)

Staff member: Lucas, maybe you weren't, and now I'd like you to focus on me as you will need this for the activity you will be doing next, thanks.

So how does this work? Rather than the member of staff challenging the pupil and escalating the problem, which would distract learning further for both Lucas and other children, the staff member focuses on redirecting the pupil by to the learning.

The 'maybe' part of the script works because it is a partial agreement; the staff member is not saying that Lucas is wrong and that she saw the note, and Lucas doesn't feel as though he has been caught out and want to defend himself. The 'and' then redirects the behaviour to what is needed.

The pupil then feels validated that it is ok to continue with getting back on track, and there is no need for anyone to say anything further.

Additional books by Hook and Vass are listed in the 'Further Reading' section of the chapter.

Reflect

Consider the strategies around the use of verbal language, and choose two strategies to try out in the next week such as using clear instructions, using pupil names or using the maybe…and…script. Sometimes it may feel uncomfortable trying out new language and scripts, but once they become embedded as another tool for you to use, they flow more easily.

The School Behaviour Policy: the Impact for Neurodivergent Pupils

You may have heard of the term 'behaviourism', the term originated in the late 1800s when Edward Thorndyke researched the behaviour of animals. He demonstrated that cats could make a link between pressing a lever and releasing themselves from being enclosed in a box and receiving a treat. Following this, Burrhus Frederick Skinner introduced the phrase 'operant conditioning' and applied this in a class full of students, giving praise when they answered questions correctly.

Ivan Pavlov was working at a similar time and developed the term 'classical conditioning' in which he made connections of dogs salivating when they heard the footsteps of the person brining them food. He made links with positive associations and rewards, and negative associations and sanctions. This is closely aligned with how behaviourism has transferred into our education system that we see today.

You will be able to see behaviourism in your school and within the school policy. It will be embedded throughout practice, and it has its place within the education system as it is effective and works for the majority of pupils, the majority of the time. It is a simple and effective way of managing behaviour in the classroom. However, strategies such as this may be ineffective for our neurodivergent pupils due to the underlying processing difference and co-occurrences. In fact, using strategies such as these could be detrimental to our neurodivergent pupils; for example, we now know so much more about SPD, and trying to apply a behaviourism model may not get to the underlying need and support a pupil might require. Or, it may cause them to 'mask' their true feelings and behaviours and bottle this up until a time that they feel safe, such as reaching home at the end of the day, and commonly when parents say that their neurodivergent child acts differently and 'melts down'.

The Use of Isolation

Some schools (particularly secondary schools) may use isolation rooms. This is used when a child breaches a behaviour policy. It is a room in which a pupil will sit and do their work away from other pupils. It may also be called a reset or reflection room. The Independent Provider of Special Education Advice (IPSEA) (2022) states that the use of this type of room in a mainstream school is completely inappropriate for neurodivergent pupils. It argues that 'it is never appropriate to place pupils with SEND in a removal room as a punishment. As well as not being inclusive practice, these rooms are not settings for specialist intervention and support for a child or young person with SEND'.

The DfE (2016) states in its publication *Behaviour and Discipline in Schools: Advice for Headteachers and School Staff*:

> The use of seclusion/isolation rooms: As with all other disciplinary penalties, schools must act reasonably in all circumstances when using such rooms.

(see paragraphs 14 and 15)

15. A punishment must be proportionate. In determining whether a punishment is reasonable, section 91 of the Education and Inspections Act 2006 says the penalty must be reasonable in all the circumstances and that **account must be taken of the pupil's age, any special educational needs or disability they may have**, and any religious requirements affecting them.

Use of an isolation room may be out of your control, and form part of school policy. But, when working with your neurodivergent pupils, think how things could be done differently, and have you taken into account their SEND needs. For example, can you explore what the trigger was to their behaviour first? Can you discuss and reflect on the behaviour with the pupil and the impact on others? Can you discuss the longer term impact if their behaviour continues in this way? Are there any interventions around social skills that could be introduced?

As you develop your behaviour management skills, you will also develop your own ethos around this. Your ethos may be influenced by many aspects such as your own schooling and how you were managed by teachers. Although you may not be able to influence policy or strategies used, your opinion should be valued as a professional working with pupils and offer alternative strategies and solutions as you progress with your training, as you may come into contact with new areas that other staff may not have read about yet.

Working with Parents and Carers

Chapter 8 will look in depth at working with parents and carers, but at this stage it is important to note that working with parents and carers is really important in developing consistency with behaviour management. You may need to build relationships with parents and carers who are reluctant to come into school or who are having their own challenges with their child if you work closely with a pupil, or if the class teacher is out of the school ons a training course for example, then it may be appropriate that you catch up with a parent at the start or end of the day. This may be part of your job role.

Listen carefully to parents and carers; they may suggest strategies that work for them at home that you can try in school. Or they may identify triggers or key times where a pupil might be feeling more anxious.

Internal, Fixed Term (Suspension) and Permanent Exclusions

Challenging behaviour can lead to the exclusion of a pupil. Did you know that SEND pupils with an EHCP are five times more likely to be permanently excluded than other pupils? That is quite an alarming number. The figures do not include pupils with undiagnosed SEND needs either. Often, a pupil is excluded due to unmet needs of the pupil and the school not having the resources to support the pupil. The pupil may need a more specialist provision, but places and funding for these places are very much in short supply.

There are three types of exclusions: internal, fixed term (suspension) and permanent exclusions.

Internal Exclusion

An internal exclusion is when a pupil is removed from being taught directly in their normal class(es) They will have a fixed period of time (from a few hours up to a few days) in which they will carry out their learning activities in another part of the school. They will stay on the school site.

Fixed Term Exclusion (Suspension)

A fixed term exclusion or suspension is when a pupil is excluded from the school site for a fixed period of time, for example, between one to three days. The pupil will spend this time at home and should not be out in public during this time. School staff and parents or carers will have a meeting on the pupil's return and discuss any further adjustments that may need to be made and the expectations for the pupil.

Permanent Exclusion

A permanent exclusion may be used when there are persistent breaches of the behaviour policy, or if this has been a single incident of a serious nature. The permanent exclusion must be reviewed by members of the Governing Body, and the parents or carers are invited to attend this and present their views. If the exclusion is upheld by the governors, then the parents or carers can appeal this decision.

Alternatives to an Exclusion Approach: Developing a Place of Belonging for Your Neurodivergent Pupils

As we saw from the figures in the above section, it is concerning that so many neurodivergent pupils are excluded. So how can we work to develop a different approach in schools?

The National Education Union (NEU) (2022) examined the place of belonging and building a community in schools to support pupils. In schools where this was successful the following was found:

- There was common positive language and practice shared by all school staff.
- A belonging approach was applied to the behaviour management strategy.
- There were fewer sanctions used.
- There were more approaches based around interventions and valuing individuals.

What might this look like in your class or school?

Chapter Summary

This chapter has looked at some general behaviour management strategies and the use of behaviourism in schools, and it has also focused on specific approaches for neurodivergent pupils such as considering some strategies for anxiety and ODD. It has also questioned the use of isolation rooms and exclusions for neurodivergent pupils.

Glossary of Key Terms

- Fixed term exclusion or suspension – a short-term exclusion in which the pupil stays at home and returns after the fixed period ends.
- Internal exclusion – a short-term separation of a pupil from their normal class after an incident which is against the behaviour policy.
- Permanent exclusion – when there have been serious breaches of the behaviour policy, a permanent exclusion may be implemented.

Further Reading

ADHD Foundation (2021) 'SLANT' Won't Work for SEND Students, So What Does? www.adhdfoundation.org.uk/2021/09/13/slant-wont-work-for-send-students-so-what-does/.

Bennett, T. (2016) The Beginning Teacher's Behaviour Toolkit. https://tombennetttraining.co.uk/wp-content/uploads/2020/05/Tom_Bennett_summary.pdf.

Education Endowment Foundation. https://educationendowmentfoundation.org.uk/.

Hook, A. and Vass, P. (2011) *Behaviour Management Pocketbook*. Teachers' Pocketbooks. London.

Hook, A. and Vass, P. (2016) *Teaching with Influence*. David Fulton Publishers. London.

Independent Provider of Special Education Advice (IPSEA) (2022) www.ipsea.org.uk/.

O'Regan (2006) *Challenging Behaviours Pocketbook*. Teachers' Pocketbooks. London.

References

Department for Education (DfE) (2016) *Behaviour and Discipline in Schools; Advice for Headteachers and School Staff.*

Education Endowment Foundation (2019) Improving Behaviour in Schools; Six Recommendations for Improving Behaviour in Schools. https://educationendowmentfoundation.org.uk/education-evidence/guidance-reports/behaviour.

Ellis, S. and Todd, J. (2018) *Behaviour for Learning: Promoting Positive Relationships in the Classroom*. Routledge, London.

Hook, A. and Vass, P. (2016) *Teaching with Influence*. David Fulton Publishers. London.

Independent Provider of Special Education Advice (IPSEA) (2022) www.ipsea.org.uk/.

Mould, K. (2020) 'Learning Behaviours' Are About More Than Managing Misbehaviour in the Classroom. https://educationendowmentfoundation.org.uk/news/eef-blog-what-are-effective-learning-behaviours-and-how-can-we-develop-them.

National Education Union (NEU) (2022) SEND Students and Exclusions. https://neu.org.uk/send-students-and-exclusion.

Reflect

Think back to Chapter 3. What behaviour challenges have you been experiencing with your neurodivergent pupils? Have you been able to practise some strategies that you chose in the 'reflect and implement' activity or implement something new for one of your neurodivergent pupils?

4 Pupil Well-Being and Neurodiversity

Chapter Aims

- To gain an understanding of well-being in the classroom context and how this might impact your neurodivergent pupils.
- To understand the importance of pupil happiness and resilience in your classroom.
- To gain an understanding of the impact of anxiety on your neurodivergent pupils and consider strategies to support them.
- To begin to explore some common areas of mental health that impact your neurodivergent pupils such as depression.
- To begin to have an overview of the meaning of adverse childhood experiences (ACEs) and trauma, and where to find further support and training.

Links to the Professional Standards for Teaching Assistants

Personal and Professional Conduct

- **1 Having personal and professional regard for the ethos, policies and practices of the school** in which they work as professional members of staff.
- **2 Demonstrating positive attitudes, values and behaviours** to develop and sustain effective relationships with the school community.
- **3 Having regard for the need to safeguard pupils' well-being** by following relevant statutory guidance along with school policies and practice.
- **5 Committing to improve their own practice** through self-evaluation and awareness.

DOI: 10.4324/9781003427599-5

Knowledge and Understanding

- **1 Acquire the appropriate skills, qualifications and/or experience** required for the teaching assistant role with support from the school employer.
- **2 Demonstrate expertise and skills in understanding the needs of all pupils** (including specialist expertise as appropriate) and know how to adapt and deliver support to meet individual needs.
- **3 Share responsibility for ensuring that their own knowledge and understanding is relevant and up to date** by reflecting on their own practice, liaising with school leaders and accessing relevant professional development to improve personal effectiveness.
- **5 Understand their roles and responsibilities within the classroom and whole school context** recognising that these may extend beyond a direct support role.

Teaching and Learning

- **3** Use effective behaviour management strategies consistently in line with the school's policy and procedures.
- **5** Communicate effectively and sensitively with pupils to adapt to their needs and support their learning.

Working with Others

- **1 Recognise and respect the role and contribution of other professionals, parents and carers** by liaising effectively and working in partnership with them.

- **2 With the class teacher, keep other professionals accurately informed** of progress or concerns they may have about the pupils they work with.
- **3 Understand their responsibility to share knowledge** to inform planning and decision-making.
- **4 Understand their role** in order to be able to work collaboratively with classroom teachers and other colleagues, including specialist advisory teachers.
- **5 Communicate their knowledge and understanding of pupils** to other school staff and education, health and social care professionals so that informed decision-making can take place on intervention and provision.

Introduction

Pupil well-being is a vital area to be explored in schools at this current time. It is a high priority on government agenda, and there are particular concerns following the impact of the pandemic. Pupils are affected by life events in different ways, and social, emotional and mental health (SEMH) needs can also co-exist with other neurodiverse differences and is common in areas such as autism and attention-deficit hyperactivity disorder (ADHD).

It is concerning that research has indicated that neurodivergent pupils are much more likely to have lower self-esteem, feel more anxious or depressed and be generally less happy or content than neurotypical pupils. These pupils are more likely to have co-occurring mental health needs. For example, autistic pupils are more like to experience depression and/or anxiety, and dyslexic pupils are more likely to experience low self-esteem.

In addition to neurodivergent pupils, it is also important to consider pupils who may be in care themselvesor looked after children, or those who are acting as a carer for a parent or sibling. These pupils are also at risk of SEMH needs. Although we wouldn't class these pupils as being neurodivergent, elements of this chapter will be equally as important and applicable to them too. It is important to seek out information from schools to see if there is any additional policy or guidance in school that you need to be aware of; for example, is there a carer's policy? For other pupils, they may have a physical disability or chronic illness and have associate SEMH needs.

The Department for Education (DfE) (2022) issued guidance for supporting the mental health of pupils in schools and colleges. It focuses on developing whole school approaches and strategies to support all pupils. Training is offered on the early signs of mental well-being concerns; Relationships, Sex and Health Education (RSHE); and where and how to seek support. If you would like to develop your expertise in this area, then do seek out specific training and courses and become a champion for mental health and well-being in your school for your pupils.

The government has gone a step further recently and has outlined targets to have mental health teams situated in schools. The teams will be responsible for supporting and delivering early intervention from evidence-informed practices and provide the expertise and capacity in school.

Professional Discussion

What expertise around mental health for pupils is available in your school? Is there any specific training that is advised? Do you have a mental health team located in your school yet? If so, what does their support and provision look like?

Neurodivergent Pupils and Poor Mental Health and Well-Being: the Connection

There are many reasons why neurodivergent pupils may be experiencing poor mental health, challenges and issues. Pupils may have underlying factors that are associated with their challenges as a neurodivergent individual. For example, a pupil may find a particular task difficult and notice that the majority of their neurotypical peers do not face the same challenges or need to put in as much effort as they do. This, in turn, may have a negative effect on the pupil's self-esteem.

We know that some neurodivergent pupils may have particular difficulties in areas such as communication, which can have a detrimental effect on developing and maintaining friendships. Because of this, pupils may be lacking in friendship groups that they can talk through their own problems with or look for peer support. These friendship groups often come up with solutions to problems or demonstrate to individuals that they are not the only one going through some of these difficulties, but if our neurodivergent pupils do not have these same social circles, they can feel isolated which can contribute further to their mental health issues.

Some neurodivergent pupils may have difficulty with tasks that peers of their own age are carrying out and developing their own sense of self, belonging and independence. For example, pupils may not be able to go out alone or use public transport. They therefore fall even further away from their potential social network and peer support system.

All of the factors above may have a negative impact on the pupil, isolate them and contribute to them becoming more vulnerable to bullying. It is therefore incredibly important for this to be closely monitored by all staff, and within your role as a member of support staff, as neurodivergent pupils will often build strong relationships with adults rather than their peer groups.

What Does SEMH Look Like?

SEMH needs may range in severity, some pupils may have what appears to be milder needs or support and others may have more serious and long-term mental health conditions. Each child will present differently depending on their mental health profile of needs and their co-occurring differences. All staff need to be vigilant and look out for the following signs of mental health issues in their pupils:

- A pupil becoming more withdrawn than what is their normal behaviour
- Angry or violent behaviour
- The appearance of being depressed
- Anxiety (discussed in further detail later in the chapter)
- Resentment towards other pupils or family members
- Having low self-esteem

- Not wanting to come to school and become a school-refuser
- Showing signs of self-harming
- Taking drugs or alcohol misuse
- Participating in risk-taking behaviours such as hanging out with older pupils or participating in illegal activities

Mental health can have an impact on pupils underachieving, missing school, being excluded or having the positive peer relationships that they need.

The Importance of Pupil Happiness

The Autism Education Trust (AET) provide a framework for working with autistic pupils; this can be applied to other areas of neurodiversity. It highlights within their mission and values that the most important element is pupil well-being.

Young experts from AET (2022) state, 'When supporting us at school, the focus should be on well-being, not conformity', which is a powerful statement from the autistic community. The AET supports this through their vision which includes 'Our vision is a world where all autistic children and young people experience a positive education that supports well-being' leading to **'empower the education workforce and support them in securing a positive education that supports well-being for all** autistic children and young people'. Your role as a teaching assistant (TA) or learning support assistant (LSA) is vital in ensuring that you are empowered to do this for all neurodivergent pupils that you work with.

The AET outlines ways in which this can be done – consider how this applies to your own role in school and how it is applicable to neurodivergent pupils:

- Share knowledge and understanding.
- Develop your skills as part of the workforce.
- Embed positive attitudes towards neurodiversity.
- Gain support from system leaders.

The aim of AET is to lead to outcomes such as an increase in pupils that receive appropriate support in school and have a positive educational experience and for neurodivergent pupils to feel empowered and be able to self-advocate.

Happiness means different things to different people. Think about this scenario but for two different people attending a gig for a favourite band. For one person this may bring about a sense of excitement, fulfilment and enjoyment for a band that they have a particular special interest or focus on, but for another, the crowded area and noise may cause anxiety or the need to withdraw. Either could be applied to someone neurodivergent, which is why it is important to remember to consider the wider elements of impact upon an individual.

Happiness can be seen in different forms: it could be through the indication of something that has brought joy through an event or achievement on a short-term basis, or it could be a sense of contentment over a much longer period of time.

Professional Discussion

What strategies are in place in your school that support pupil happiness? Can you suggest any strategies that would support your neuorodivergent pupil's happiness in school?

The Use of Therapy Dogs in Schools

The use of therapy dogs in schools is becoming more popular with many schools, particularly primary schools training their own therapy dogs as part of the school team. The School Therapy Dog Association (link in the 'Further Reading' section of the chapter) supports the use of therapy dogs to help promote the well-being of pupils. Pupils work to develop relationships with the dogs through caring for them, training them and taking responsibility for their needs. This can have a positive effect on pupils wanting to attend to school (in the case of school-refusers and pupils with anxiety and attachment issues). The therapy dog also provides the opportunity for pupils to spend time with them, for someone to talk to who doesn't react in the same way an adult does, or for an adult to use the therapy dog in order to demonstrate or initiate conversations around boundaries and behaviours that need tackling.

Paul (2019) argues for the need of every school to have a therapy dog. This would support mental health and well-being for the children most in need and become an active member of the school community and support team. He argues, 'just with the presence of a therapy dog within a classroom, medical science has shown that a therapy dog can reduce blood pressure, promote physical healing, reduce anxiety, fatigue and depression, as well as provide emotional support'. So why not have a therapy dog? The majority of schools will not have a therapy dog, as a dog needs looking after outside school hours and this takes commitment from a member of the senior leadership team. There are procedures in place to have a dog in school, such as dog training that is specific for schools and requirements for insurance.

Does your school have a therapy dog? If not, do any of your local schools have one? Find out if you can make a visit to see the therapy dog in action, and talk with staff about the benefits.

Common Mental Health Issues

Anxiety

Anxiety can lead to an anxiety attack. There is a difference between what we know are anxiety attacks and what are categorised as panic attacks. An anxiety attack is when the anxiety is related to something that is happening or about to happen; it relates to the current situation. A panic attack is when someone has an attack at any time, but it is normally unrelated to their current situation, so the trigger may be unknown or related to a separate situation.

Both anxiety attacks and panic attacks may present with the same or similar physical symptoms and could include some or all of the following:

- A dry mouth
- Racing heartbeat or palpitations
- Hyperventilating
- The need to go to the toilet
- Churning or butterflies feeling in the stomach
- Nausea or sickness

Let's look at anxiety in further detail.

There are two types of anxiety:

- Generalised anxiety, also known as Generalised Anxiety Disorder (GAD)
- Phobias, which can be broken down into further types of phobias:

  - Specific phobia: a fear of something specific such as spiders or the dark
  - Social phobia: a fear of being embarrassed in a social situation
  - School phobia; a fear of going to school, which could be linked with social phobia
  - Agoraphobia: a fear of leaving the house and being in a public space
  - Separation anxiety: a fear of being left
  - Selective mutism: severe social anxiety, which results in the loss of the ability to speak in stressful situations

These will affect pupils in different in ways, for example:

- With a specific phobia, pupils may avoid situations where they may come into contact with their phobia and not want to go out onto the field to play as there may be bees or other insects.
- Pupils may not want to come into school or leave the classroom if they have a social phobia as they are too frightened to speak in front of others in the class, do a presentation or read aloud.
- A phobia of school itself could be linked with an incidence of bullying.
- A pupil may become distressed when being separated from a parent and is often seen in younger pupils.

- When pupils lose the ability to speak, although it is labelled as selective mutism, it is a physical reaction to a stressful situation and the pupil has no control over this.

Pupil behaviour can be affected in a variety of ways due to anxiety or phobias. They may avoid coming to school, walk or run out of class to avoid a situation or refuse to do something that would result in them being caused further anxiety.

It is important to identify triggers to pupil anxiety so that they can be approached in a supportive way, and the right support or strategies are used with the pupil. Triggers could include:

Triggers inside the classroom:

- Insects getting inside the classroom
- Being asked to read aloud to the class
- Discussing something in front of the whole class or being asked questions
- Tests or exams

Triggers outside the classroom:

- The weather outside, for example, story weather
- Large open spaces
- Noisy, crowded communal areas (as discussed in Chapter 2)
- Using school toilets due to the germs

Wider potential triggers:

- Vaccinations
- The fear of being sick or catching an illness another pupil may have
- Travelling on public transport: buses, trains or the underground
- Using lifts or escalators

Some of the wider potential triggers may need consideration when planning for a school trip. Consider some strategies to implement for pupils that are anxious.

Preparation for Lessons

Reflect

How do you prepare pupils for lessons that are coming up that day?

Prepare pupils for lessons through talking with them so that they can visualise what the lesson may include. You may include the use of a visual timetable or instructions, or a breakdown of the lesson. You may need to go a step further than the use of a visual timetable as they may need further information such as what equipment may be being used and how confident they are using this. Or what tasks or activities may be included within the lesson, such as group work, or feeding back to the class. How could they be supported further with these tasks? Ensure that you give your neurodivergent pupils the time to check in with you throughout lessons to clarify information or for you to prepare them for the next stage in the lesson.

Routines are good for neurodivergent pupils, but sometimes changes in the school day cannot be predicted. How can you support pupils with these unexpected changes? Sometimes pupils may need extra time to adjust to the changes.

The use of social stories is a good way to help your pupils prepare for upcoming changes such as transitions to new classes and year groups, or going on a school trip, or lesson projects that fall outside of the normal lesson structures. There are some very good resources and books on social stories, and when done well, they are very effective. There is further guidance on social stories in the 'Further Reading' section at the end of the chapter.

Ensure that you explain any rules carefully. Communication can break down and cause anxiety when it is thought that a pupil has broken a rule or is not following a rule; however, this could be due to a lack of understanding as outlined in the short case study below.

Case Study

Hudson was seven years old. He had some delay of his speech development and was showing indications of autism. He was awaiting further assessment, but the school was supporting him through anIndividual Education Plan (IEP) and specific strategies for difficulties and challenges that arose.

There had been an incident in which the class teacher had asked the pupils to ensure that they were following their rule: 'Be respectful to your friends and your classroom'. Hudson had been rough with some equipment and broken it. The teacher had reminded Hudson of the rule; however, the same thing happened just a few hours later.

At the end of the day, Hudson's mother was called in to class. The teacher, Hudson, his LSA and Hudson's mother sat down to talk about the incidents. On questioning, Hudson's mother realised that there was a problem with the way in which Hudson was agreeing that he had been told the rule. His mother asked him to explain what the rule meant, and Hudson repeated the rule but couldn't explain it. Hudson had no understanding of what the word 'respectful' meant. Although the teacher said she had explored the word at the start of the term, Hudson had not processed this, not understood it or forgotten it. So, he carried on with the behaviour.

Reflect

Consider how you might communicate better with a neurodivergent pupil in your class(es) Have you had any difficulty with them not understanding a rule? Can you break down rules and reason for them any differently, or more regularly?

We are now going to look at a case study that focuses on the processes of support for a pupil demonstrating anxiety.

Case Study

From a School Pastoral Lead LSA

The class teacher was becoming increasingly concerned for one of his pupils, Ramon. Ramon was starting to refuse to come into class in the morning, and it was causing his mum to become upset and the start of the day was very unsettled.

The teacher approached the pastoral lead in the school to ask for some advice on how to handle the situation. The first step taken was to monitor the situation, to note carefully what was happening and to work out why it might be happening. At the same time, the TA in his class was asked to have a series of conversations with Ramon at different times, one directly as the drop-off was happening, another after and another later in the day. This was to see whether Ramon could explain what he was feeling and thinking at the time, or soon after the event, or to give an opportunity for Ramon to explain later in the day once he had calmed down. The TA was very careful not to escalate the situation, but to encourage Ramon to identify and share what was happening for him (if possible) so that they could gain further information on how to support him.

There could have been a range of factors affecting Ramon and impacting on him coming in to school, such as an issue at home – for example, a parental split, bereavement, loss of a pet or changes within the home structure – or an issue within school – for example, anxiety over a lesson or area of learning, or issues with friendships or a particular pupil.

The pastoral lead also made a telephone call to Ramon's mum to have a discussion around what they thought could be happening and to see if they had contacted anyone about this such as their GP General Practitioner (Doctor) or made a referral to Child and Adolescent Mental Health Services (CAMHS) for support.

Triangulating the information gathering ensured that as much information that could be sought was sought, before any decisions on the next steps were taken. For Ramon, it appeared that there was a problem with his current friendship group. Ramon had a diagnosis of autism, and this was an area that he struggled with at times, although staff hadn't noticed any current issues.

From this, the class teacher and pastoral lead had a conversation with the Special Educational Needs Co-ordinator to discuss what provision or interventions may be available to support Ramon. They decided to look at the internal provisions first, with the knowledge that CAMHS might be an option at a later date if needed.

The support implemented included:

1. Giving Ramon time to talk:, this was 1:1 with the class TA.
2. Therapy walks three times a week with the TA and the school support dog.
3. Ramon was added to the waiting list for a group intervention with the learning mentor to manage and discuss his feelings.
4. Modelling and implementing mindfulness strategies to support self-regulation and calmness when feelings of anxiety were triggered.
5. The use of the breakfast club to give Ramon additional time to come in in the morning and talk first thing if needed without the additional pressure of the start of the school day.
6. The use of the nurture group at break and lunch time with supported facilitation of friendships to widen Ramon's friendship group which was facilitated by staff.

The school was a large, well-resourced school, with many interventions and support groups running at all times which supported a range of strategies for Ramon.

Reflect

In the above case study, there were many interventions and support strategies that could be offered to Ramon. This might be different in your own setting as some interventions may depend on money, resourcing and time. Consider if Ramon was a pupil in your class: what strategies and support might be available in your school? What process might need to be put in place for you to access additional support for Ramon?

Depression

We all experience feeling sad, or feeling a bit low or down at times, and this is normal. Not everything is great in life all of the time unfortunately. Feeling low can vary at different times of our lives and for a huge variety of reasons. It can even vary across an individual week or month. However, we need to become more concerned if we find that this period of being low becomes more persistent or starts to feel overwhelming. We need to look out for this with our pupils.

It is always important that if we suspect depression in a pupil, those concerns are referred to a pastoral team. They will be able to discuss these concerns with parents or carers and advise on the next steps. Depression responds well to a variety of medical treatments and support, and it is therefore important to pass information on so that pupils can gain this support if needed.

There are potentially many reasons that could cause an episode of depression, which include:

- A pupil feeling lonely or isolated.
- Extreme adverse circumstances in a pupil's life such as trauma, abuse, bereavement or illness.
- Hormonal changes.
- Identity developments and changes such as gender, sexuality, cultural or religious.

It is common for depression to co-exist with other neurodiverse differences such as ADHD or autism spectrum condition.

What are some of the signs of depression that you may see in your pupils?

- Unusual low moods that don't seem to disappear
- A pupil being self-critical
- Lacking energy and not engaging in normal class or school activities that they would normally join
- Being irritable or angry
- Neglecting their own personal hygiene
- Loss of appetite
- Lack of sleep, which you may see through the pupil being tired in class
- The pupil participating in risky behaviours
- Self-harming

Obsessive-Compulsive Disorder

Obsessive-compulsive disorder (OCD) is a common mental health difference. We saw in Chapter 1 that OCD can present itself as obsessive thoughts and anxiety around certain situations. It can include the compulsion to carry out particular activities and routines so that the person feels safe. Often there are compulsions such as hand washing, the cleaning of surfaces or repeating things in a ritualistic way such as locking a door several times or checking that appliances are turned off.

If younger pupils have OCD, research shows that this tends to decrease as they get older. However, OCD can be extremely debilitating and affect pupil attendance in school or the ability to complete homework. Pupils may not only feel embarrassed about their compulsion but also feel that they have little control over stopping them due to the anxiety this would cause.

Pupils with OCD should be getting further support from Mental Health professionals. School support staff need to consider what their role may be in supporting pupils with OCD. This may include setting or supporting work that a pupil is doing at home if they have been unable to come into school. If a pupil is in school, then support around anxiety may need to be given, or additional time for a pupil to carry out rituals to ensure that they are ready to carry out the school tasks.

Post-Traumatic Stress Disorder

Post-traumatic stress disorder (PTSD) can be caused by fear or anxiety for a child that has continued over a long period of time. A pupil may become withdrawn, or they are likely to have a high sense of hyperarousal, in which they are in a constant state of fight or flight. Research has shown that children who are exposed to traumatic experiences when young may have brain developmental changes in order to react to the constant fear and survival needed.

Pupils with PTSD may show symptoms such as:

- Difficulty in explaining or understanding their feelings.
- Difficulty in making friends or maintaining friendships.
- The inability to trust adults.
- The lack of the sense of safety.
- Becoming angry easily.
- Poor concentration.
- Being fearful of failing.

What strategies will support pupils with PTSD? PTSD is complex, and time, support and additional care will be needed with pupils. There may be a range of health professionals supporting your pupil, and they may need additional support and understanding in the classroom. This could include development and intervention around self-esteem, giving additional time to listen to them using active listening techniques (outlined in the 'Further Reading' section of the chapter), further support from a pastoral team, opportunities for your pupil to release frustration or anger through sport during break and lunch times or the use of mindfulness techniques through whole class work or individual support.

ACEs and Trauma

There are three types of ACEs that relate to combined traumatic events that have a significant impact:

1 Acute: this relates to a one-off incident or event such as the death of a pet.
2 Chronic: this is through repeated exposure to an experience such as witnessing domestic violence.
3 Complex: this is when there is a very personal or invasive nature to the trauma and can include abuse, neglect, death of a parent or a parent being in prison.

Chronic and complex experiences and trauma are likely to have a lasting impact on pupils, and pupils may need long-term support and therapy work.

How Do ACEs Affect Pupils in School?

ACEs could affect pupil cognitive development and therefore their learning. As we have mentioned earlier, trauma can impact on brain development, with the fight or flight mode for survival being the most important job. Therefore, other cognitive functions may not be as effective, and this could present as challenges with new learning or retaining information. Strategies to support memory could be implemented, and learning theories such as dual coding could be useful.

There could also be an impact on executive functioning, which is also a key challenge for your autistic and ADHD pupils. This will impact on organisation and planning and carrying out daily tasks.

The impact of ACEs could greatly affect pupil trust with adults and in turn affect relationships and present with challenging behaviour.

Reflect

Pupils with ACEs will need a great deal of support. Consider your role as a member of support staff: what might your involvement look like in supporting your pupil in the following areas?

- To develop resilience
- To cope with stressful situations
- To be supported by a safe community
- To be embraced by a welcome and safe environment
- Preparation for any changes

Pupils will also need support from a loving family and home environment, and guidance on how to repair relationships when they break down.

Further strategies could also be useful that have been discussed for neurodivergent differences, such as those outlined in Chapter 2 and include:

- Creative therapies.
- Sensory experiences such as sand and water play.
- The use of music to change the mood such as to energise or to calm.
- Using a weighted blanket.

Activity

Find out if there is training on ACEs and trauma in your school or hub. Who is able to access this, and can you attend? For some schools, it could be compulsory for all staff; for others, it will just be teaching staff.

It can be very difficult as an LSA or TA to access training via your school if your contract hours do not include time to access additional training. However, it is vital if you are working with pupils with specific needs that you are given the time to be trained and extend your knowledge in these areas.

General Supporting Strategies

Highlight any of the following general supporting strategies that you use in your class and the wider school to support pupil mental health and well-being. Are there any additional strategies that you can add to the list that haven't been included?

- Develop opportunities for pupils to recognise their strengths.
- Include activities that pupils really enjoy and enthuse about.
- Identify and celebrate what is going well for your pupils.
- Celebrate difference within your classroom.
- Opportunities for pupils to try new things and experience what they might be good at.
- Don't make assumptions about how pupils are feeling; ask them.
- Develop resilience.
- Normalise failure.
- Develop independence.
- Use active listening.
- Use displays to promote positive mental health.
- Offer nurture groups.
- Host well-being weeks.
- Anything else that you have seen specifically?
- Add your own strategy to the list here
- Add your own strategy to the list here.

Your school may have specific focused group activities that support the development of describing and naming feelings or managing feelings. It may include elements such as understanding how their own behaviour affects other people such as their peers, staff or parents. Groups may include developing strategies to work on how they develop skills to pick themselves up after failing something or tackling changes or transitions.

Well-Being and School Policy

Some schools will have a separate well-being policy; for others, it may be a section within another policy such as the special educational needs and disabilities or behaviour policy; or for some schools, this may still be in development or not exist at all.

Well-being is such an important area, and the impact of COVID on mental health and the closure of schools, facilities and lockdowns is very much apparent and visible in pupils in school. School should have a well-being policy and demonstrate commitment, and clear vision and values in this area and may include setting out aims and the purpose such as to promote positive mental health, how pupils with mental health needs are supported and what training is available for staff. It could include an overview of strategies: promoting and creating a sense of belonging for all pupils, promoting pupil voice, celebrating pupil achievement, both academic and non-academic, and how to seek support for individual needs.

Activity

Find out whether your school has a separate well-being policy. What does this look like? Or is there a section included within another policy or as part of an action plan instead? Can you see the policy being implemented within your school or class?

Supporting Parents with Pupils' Mental Health Needs

Parents may be reluctant to seek mental health support for the child as they associate negative stigma with mental health, or they may fear being blamed for mental health issues that their child has. It might be that the parent sees a different child at home to how school views a child. For example, a child who behaves well in school may have been struggling internally all day, and then feel relaxed at home and be able to express themselves more easily through more challenging behaviour. It could be the opposite, in which the child has presented challenges at school, but once at home feels relaxed and safe and is able to calm down. This is why it is incredibly important to discuss parental concerns, perceptions and viewpoints and to ensure that they are passed on. As an LSA or TA, you may have frequent conversations with parents or carers, and you need to share any information that is given to you. Is there a recording method in your class(es) for doing so? A book to note things down, or somewhere to log a message? In a secondary school, you may not have as much contact with parents, but you may still have some contact during a handover or to discuss an issue or concern.

Your pastoral team will be able to offer some support. They may advise parents to seek specialist help from a doctor or other medical advisor, a school mentor or a counsellor, or they may refer the pupil to a youth support or counselling team, particularly if a pupil is becoming involved in risky behaviour.

The pastoral team may refer to other services such as the CAMHS from the local mental health care team, or if the family are working with social care, then information may be passed to them.

Further resources are highlighted at the end of this chapter.

Chapter Summary

This chapter has explored mental health and well-being of pupils. You have started to think about your role in school and how this relates to this aspect of support, and the variety of mental health needs that may be present in your classes. Use the resources below to carry out additional reading or to seek further guidance and training.

Glossary of Key Terms

- Dual coding – using different types of stimuli to support learners to encode, store and retrieve information easier
- Executive functioning – a set of skills including using working memory, task switching and organisation

Further Reading and Supporting Resources

Reading

- Bomber, L. (2007) *Inside I'm hurting*. Worth Publishing. Broadway.
- Cairns, K. and Cairns, B. (2016) *Attachment, Trauma and Resilience*. CoramBAAF. London.
- Geddes, H. (2006) *Attachment in the Classroom: A Practical Guide for Schools*. Worth Publishing. Broadway.

Resources

- Anxiety UK. www.anxietyuk.org.uk/get-help/support-for-children-young-people/.
- Autism Education Trust (AET) (2022). www.autismeducationtrust.org.uk/.
- Centre for Disease Control and Prevention (2022) Communicating with Your Child; Active Listening. www.cdc.gov/parents/essentials/communication/activelistening.html.

- Department for Education (DfE) (2021) Mental Health Well-being Resources for Teachers and Teaching Staff. https://assets.publishing. service.gov.uk/government/uploads/system/uploads/attachment_data/ file/993669/Mental_Health_Resources_for_teachers_and_teaching_staff_ June_2021.pdf.
- The Mix, Mental Health Support for under 25s. www.themix.org.uk/ mental-health.
- OCD Youth. https://ocdyouth.org/.
- Place2Be, Children's Mental Health. www.place2be.org.uk/.
- School Therapy Dog Association. www.schooltherapydog.com/.
- Selective Mutism. www.selectivemutism.org.uk/.
- Royal College of Psychiatrists. Mental Health Support and Guidance for Young People, Parents and Teachers. www.rcpsych.ac.uk/mental-health/ parents-and-young-people.
- Young Minds Mental Health Support. www.youngminds.org.uk/.

References

Autism Education Trust (AET) (2022) www.autismeducationtrust.org.uk/.

Department for Education (DfE) (2022) Promoting and Supporting Mental Health and Well-Being in Schools and Colleges. www.gov.uk/guidance/ mental-health-and-well-being-support-in-schools-and-colleges.

Paul, S. (2019) How Therapy Dogs are Supporting School Well-being. https:// textbookteachers.co.uk/how-therapy-dogs-are-supporting-school-well-being/.

Reflect

Reflect back on Chapter 4. In this chapter, we look at the area of assessment, consider the impact of anxiety on neurodivergent pupils during periods of assessment as we move through the chapter, and what useful strategies you could implement.

5 Supporting the Assessment Needs of Neurodivergent Pupils

Chapter Aims

- To understand the different types of assessment in school.
- To consider how assessment may impact neurodivergent pupils.
- To understand the role of the teaching assistant (TA)/learning support assistant (LSA) within assessments.
- To gain an understanding of the graduated approach and the TA/LSA and teacher's responsibility within this model.
- To gain an overview of the different assessment points within the education system.
- To examine assessment tools within schools.
- To understand access arrangements for exams and tests.

Links to the Professional Standards for Teaching Assistants

Personal and Professional Conduct

- **5 Committing to improve their own practice** through self-evaluation and awareness.

Knowledge and Understanding

- **1 Acquire the appropriate skills, qualifications and/or experience** required for the teaching assistant role with support from the school employer.
- **2 Demonstrate expertise and skills in understanding the needs of all pupils** (including specialist expertise as appropriate) and know how to adapt and deliver support to meet individual needs.
- **3 Share responsibility for ensuring that their own knowledge and understanding is relevant and up to date** by reflecting on their own practice, liaising with school leaders and accessing relevant professional development to improve personal effectiveness.

DOI: 10.4324/9781003427599-6

- **5 Understand their roles and responsibilities within the classroom and whole school context** recognising that these may extend beyond a direct support role.

Teaching and Learning

- **1** Demonstrate an informed and efficient approach to teaching and learning by adopting relevant strategies to support the work of the teacher and increase achievement of all pupils including, where appropriate, those with special educational needs and disabilities.
- **4** Contribute to effective assessment and planning by supporting the monitoring, recording and reporting of pupil progress as appropriate to the level of the role.

Working with Others

- **2 With the class teacher, keep other professionals accurately informed** of progress or concerns they may have about the pupils they work with.
- **3 Understand their responsibility to share knowledge** to inform planning and decision-making.
- **4 Understand their role** in order to be able to work collaboratively with classroom teachers and other colleagues, including specialist advisory teachers.
- **5 Communicate their knowledge and understanding of pupils** to other school staff and education, health and social care professionals so that informed decision-making can take place on intervention and provision.

Introduction

This chapter will examine the two assessment types within education covering assessment for learning: formative assessment and summative assessment. It will look at how assessment may impact our neurodivergent pupils. Assessment is an important aspect of classroom practice, and it is needed to ensure the right teaching and strategies are in place to move learners forward. However, assessment can cause anxiety and stress for all pupils, but in particular neurodivergent pupils. We will look at assessment in the classroom, the low-impact assessment types that will potentially cause less stress and anxiety and the higher stakes summative assessment types that may put additional pressures on your neurodivergent pupils. The chapter will also consider other areas that may be impacted at these assessment periods of time such as pupil well-being, self-esteem and support for them.

Assessment for Learning

Assessment for Learning is an approach to assessment that promotes the use of assessment as part of a continuous informal cycle of planning, teaching, learning, assessing, reflecting and back to planning. The focus is on progressing learning rather than measuring and grading what achievement has been made.

Assessment for learning builds assessment into lessons and tasks so that understanding can be checked and adjustments made to lessons. These assessment checks can happen:

- At the beginning of a lesson to check what pupils can remember from previous lessons and learning.
- After new learning has been introduced.
- Throughout the lesson as it progresses.
- At the end of a lesson.

Glazzard and Stones (2021a, b) break down the elements of using an assessment for learning model, and reading on this can be accessed within the 'Further Reading' section of the chapter. They discuss the type of questioning to use, addressing misconceptions, marking and giving feedback. We are now going to look at formative assessment in further detail, which is part of assessment for learning, or it can be viewed as the same as assessment for learning (depending on what you read!).

Formative Assessment

Formative assessment is the type of assessment that occurs on a regular basis: every day and even within every lesson. Consider whether you see formative assessment taking place in your class: what does this look like, and how are you involved in implementing formative assessment? What do you do with the findings from your assessments once you have gathered this information?

Formative assessment feeds into the daily planning and implementation of teaching, and plans can then be adjusted if pupils haven't understood a concept, for example. A teacher may follow up by asking specific pupils individual questions to check their understanding and then adjust their teaching accordingly in line with this to benefit the pupil. As a member of support staff, you will need to do the same when you are working with individuals or groups.

Formative assessment will include (but the list is not exhaustive):

- Asking questions: open and closed questioning could be used; ensure that you give your neurodivergent pupils thinking time to process the question, and then to formulate answers. If you do not give enough time and support, it could lead to anxiety and consequently behavioural changes.
- Quizzes: these are often classed as 'low stakes' as they can be presented in a fun and engaging way in a relaxed environment, but you can gain useful information on knowledge retention as you would if pupils were taking a test.

- Polls: again, these can be 'low stakes' as you would know who has answered which questions, but pupils' peers wouldn't, so this takes the pressure off pupils' anxiety around providing right and wrong answers.
- Self-assessment: this can give you an understanding of how a pupil is feeling in relation to what they are working on, for example, their confidence in the subject area.
- Peer assessment: this can give the opportunity to work with a peer and support from a buddy to work on improving an area. Be careful how peer assessment is used: is your neurodivergent pupil comfortable with receiving feedback from a peer? How will this affect their self-esteem?

Live monitoring of pupil progress through formative assessment gives instant results so that teaching can be modified to the needs of the pupils. But it can be tricky to implement, and as a member of support staff, it can take time to practise and understand; for example, what is the impact of your questioning? What questions are you using, why are you using these, and then what do you do with the information once you have the answers?

Case Study

From a TA Working with a Pupil with Dyscalculia on a Mathematical Problem

Yani had difficulty with numbers. One of his challenges was that he reversed numbers and would mix up the digits so that the number 62 might be read as number 26, for example. This meant that he experienced further difficulties when conducting calculations and undertaking mathematical problem solving.

Samson had been working with Yani for several weeks and wanted to strengthen Yani's procedure for checking his calculations and transferring information, as this is where he would be miscalculating.

Samson gave Yani a calculation and asked him to work through this. He asked Yani to work through the steps that had been practised, and then he asked Yani questions such as: what do we do next? Why is this helpful? Yani still missed the checking step as he wanted to rush on to the next calculation and complete the work. He felt that this was his gaol. So Sampson decided to implement a checking framework and tick off the steps Yani needed to do to ensure that he had the opportunity to check each stage and compare the calculations to check that he had not made any errors that he could correct himself.

Samson needed to support the embedding of the process so that Yani had a checking tool to prevent mistakes happening in the process, and Yani could correct himself if he noticed them.

The Engagement Model

Previously in schools, P-levels or P-scales were used to assess pupils working below the national curriculum levels or age-related expectations (ARE). The engagement model has replaced these scales and has been designed to support pupils not working at ARE.

The model uses a pupil-centred approach; it focuses on the abilities and achievements of a pupil rather than any disabilities and deficits, and therefore is ideally suited to a neurodiversity approach to assessment. This model is used alongside the graduated approach which is outlined in Graduated Approach section.

The model examines and monitors progress across the four key areas of the code of practice:

- Communication and interaction
- Cognition and learning
- Social, emotional and mental health
- Sensory and/or physical needs

This model assesses not only progress in each area but also pupil engagement in developing new skills and the pupil's progress against outcomes and targets within their Education, Health and Care Plans (EHCPs) (Watts, 2022). The engagement model is mainly seen implemented in schools with specialist provision, but speak with your class teacher or Special Educational Needs Co-ordinator (SENCo) and ask if it is implemented within your school for any pupils.

Links to further reading on the engagement model can be found at the end of this chapter.

Graduated Approach

The graduated approach is used when pupils need a different sort of approach and additional strategies to the majority of pupils within your class. This will usually include your neurodivergent pupils. The graduated approach builds on Quality First Teaching (QFT) or High Quality Teaching (HQT) which is examined further in Chapter 6. The graduated approach is comprised of a four-part cycle: assess, plan, do and review. The cycle is worked through by the class teacher, SENCo, parents and carers, and will also include your input too as a member of the support team. The cycle ensures that by exploring the needs and challenges the pupil faces, the right support for them can be identified, implemented and then reviewed and amended.

It is important to note that at the centre of this approach is the pupil and their family, and gathering their views is vital in contributing, informing and beginning this cycle.

In the past, the SENCo held responsibility for the management of all of the pupils with additional needs; however, this has changed with the newest code of practice. The responsibility is now shared, and every member of school staff has an important role to play and responsibility to hold in the development, support and progress of each pupil. The class teacher has more responsibility and has the overview of the pupils with special educational needs and disabilities (SEND) that are within their class, and the review of any support plans that have been implemented This places you as a member of support staff, a step closer to providing input and progress updates to your class teacher, and in turn supporting the review and updating of the plan.

Let's outline the stages within the graduated approach:

Stage 1 – Assess

This initial stage includes gathering information from the daily types of formative assessment so that the overview of current pupil needs and targets can be formed. It will include identification of any barriers that might be in the way of the pupil making progress that is in line with their peers.

Your class teacher will have a discussion with the pupil and their parents or carers to establish their views on any challenges that the pupil may have, and you might be involved with gathering the views of the pupil as you will have developed a strong relationship with them. The teacher will also be looking for any gaps in knowledge, understanding or skills for the pupil, and whether any further assessments that the school can provide might be beneficial at this stage. The SENCo will also consider whether any referrals to other agencies or exploration of further external assessments might be useful.

Internal school assessments and tests might include reading, spelling and maths tests; profiling tools for the assessment of speech and language challenges; communication assessments that may include looking at body language and responses to scenarios and behaviours; diagnostic assessments linked to Cognitive Abilities Tests (CATs) and the use of screening tools for the possibility of dyslexia or dyspraxia. Some of these will be explored further, later in the chapter.

Your SENCo will arrange for any of these additional assessments to take place, and there may be a waiting list within school for this depending on who is conducting the assessments, their expertise, other pupils waiting to be assessed and the workload of the person undertaking the assessment. Often these types of assessment are carried out by the SENCo themselves or a specialist member of the support staff team that have had further training in the area and the implementation of the tool or test. This is something that you might like to consider doing as part of your professional development.

There may be restrictions on some types of assessment; for example, some dyslexia screening tools can only be used with pupils over the age of seven or eight.

Stage 2 – Plan

At this stage, the information that was gathered in stage 1 is discussed, and a plan will be formulated that will include support for the pupil based upon their emerging needs. The planning process will include everyone that is part of the support network for the pupil including the pupil themselves, parents or carers, the class teacher, key worker or form tutor and the SENCo. If there are any external agencies involved in supporting the pupil, they will be included too.

Included within the plan, targets will be set that are tightly focused around specific areas that have been identified. Each target should have action steps that will be granular and support the work towards the target. It will identify what the support is, who will implement this support, who will review it and how and when it will take place. It will also include specific teaching strategies and any resources linked to this.

The plan will have a timeline with review dates set. The plan needs to be shared with everyone involved in working with the pupil, and this will include you as part of that team. If you are not included in a circulation list, ensure that you sit with your class teacher to read the plan together and to understand your role in working on the targets for any pupils that you are working with.

The plan may be presented as an Individual Education Plan (IEP), one plan, a one-page profile, a pupil passport or an individual provision map.

Activity

Find out what sort of plans your school uses. Do they have IEPs, one-plan one-page profiles, pupil passports or a range of tools and approaches? Discuss with your class teacher or SENCo why this approach is used and why it works best for the pupils in your school.

Stage 3 – Do

The responsibility of implementing the plan at this 'do' stage is held with the class teacher. The implementation should be carried out on a daily basis and provision implemented at all times. It could include strategies such as:

- QFT or HQT.
- Implementing specific individual strategies or interventions which might include 1:1 or group support in maths, English, communication or social skills.
- Directing staff to implement support or strategies such as working with the TA or LSA.
- Using formative assessment to monitor and review progress.
- Adjusting in relation to progress made.
- Communicating with the SENCo, parents and carers with the progress being made.

Stage 4 – Review

The review stage is the final stage before the process is then repeated and the cycle begins again. A meeting is held in which the targets are discussed and evaluated: where has progress been made? Have any further barriers been identified? It is an opportunity to reflect upon what is currently in place and what progress has been made.

These meetings are normally held separately and may be carried out by the SENCo, the class teacher or a combination of both of them.

In preparation for the review stage, you may be asked to contribute towards the evidence gathering to be used towards the review. This might include considering your thoughts and evidence on the following:

- Has the pupil achieved the targets set? Have you any evidence to support this?
- If a pupil has not met a target, what progress has been made towards the target?
- Which interventions have been successful?
- What changes might need to be made?

At this point, it is decided whether the pupil has made enough progress to be taken off this graduated approach or enters another cycle of assess, plan, do and review (Figure 5.1).

The following questions will need to be considered at each stage of the graduated approach cycle, and you can consider these when working with your pupils:

Stage 1 – Assess

- Is the pupil able to access the curriculum?
- Is the learning environment appropriately set up? What else could you do?
- What are the pupil's interests and strengths? How are these included?

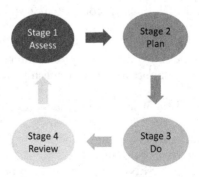

Figure 5.1 An overview model of the graduated approach as outlined in NASEN (2022).

Stage 2 – Plan

- Share any concerns with your class teacher.
- What are your pupil's views?
- How have you built on the strengths of the pupil?

Stage 3 – Do

- What has been achieved?
- What has worked well? What hasn't?

Stage 4 – Review

- What else might be useful or needed?

NASEN (2022)

Assessment Tools Used within Schools

There are a range of assessment tools used within schools. These may be used by the SENCo, specialist teacher or member of support staff such as yourself who has been trained to use the tool. It might be an area you would like to develop for yourself and become a specialist area for your own professional development.

Section 'External Professional Assessment Tools Leading to Diagnosis' will give an overview of some of the different types of assessment tools that might be used in your school and what the assessment purposes are. The tools are generally used to gain an indication of the barrier to learning for your pupil so that appropriate strategies or support can be put into place. The tools do not offer a diagnosis.

- Assessment of reading: this may come from different companies; the assessment tool will analyse the reading skills of the pupil including accuracy, fluency and comprehension. It identifies which areas a pupil needs to work on, and it may provide interventions or suggestions of resources to support this so that you could then implement them as part of your role.
- Developmental language: this assessment considers a pupil's understanding of vocabulary, grammar and the features of language.
- Dyscalculia: this assessment examines a pupil's skills in working with numbers. It identifies pupils with dyscalculia indicators and may provide interventions.
- Dyslexia: there are many dyslexia screening tools, and your school will have decided on one. The assessment tool will measure working memory, integration memory, phonological processing and decoding skills.
- Emotional literacy: these assessments will focus on self-awareness, regulation, empathy and social skills. They may include taking information from the pupil, parent or carer and the teacher to look at each perspective.

- Reasoning: there are two types of reasoning assessments: non-verbal reasoning assessments assess process and reasoning skills and are linked with progress in maths and science, and verbal reasoning assessments assess verbal thinking, logical reasoning and vocabulary.
- Recall: assessments of recall identify any cognitive difficulties relating to memory including working memory, visuo-spatial recognition and executive functioning.
- Vocabulary scale: this tool focuses on a pupil's receptive vocabulary. It will assess what a pupil is hearing and what they understand from this information.

It is important to remember that these tools will not give a diagnosis; however, they do give an indication of the neuro-differences that pupils have and will provide direction to useful strategies to support your neurodivergent pupils.

Professional Discussion

Discuss with your SENCo or class teacher what assessment tools are used in your school, who delivers them and how they are trained in the use of them, and consider your own next steps for professional development relating to this area.

External Professional Assessment Tools Leading to Diagnosis

It is never the place of a teacher, SENCo or member of the school to give a diagnosis to a child, parent or carer. As educational professionals, we can look at the behaviour a child is showing or the challenges that they are facing, and put in to places strategies to support these elements, but it is not for us to diagnose. So, who does diagnose and what does this look like?

The three more common forms of neurodiversity seen in schools are autism, attention-deficit hyperactivity disorder (ADHD) and dyslexia, and for a diagnosis of one of these, a child would need referring to a paediatric team. This could be through a general practitioner or via the school. There could be long waiting times to see a specialist, up to 18 months or longer in some cases. If a parent seeks a private assessment, then there could be expensive costs involved of approximately £2,000.

When a child is referred for an assessment, it is an assessment, not a diagnosis. A child is being assessed and may not be given a diagnosis at all.

Regardless of this, the strategies that you will be putting into place in school will still be the same for that particular pupil with or without a diagnosis, as the pupil's needs will be the same whether they have a formal diagnosis or not.

Who does the assessment?

- Autism/autism spectrum condition: the most common type of assessment for autism in the UK is the Autism Diagnostic Observation Schedule, which is a group of assessments that look at communication and social interaction, play and imagination. There is normally a team of professionals carrying out this assessment, and they discuss their findings as a team. The team may include a paediatrician, a psychologist and a speech and language therapist.
- ADHD: this assessment is normally carried out by a consultant psychiatrist.
- Dyslexia: assessments are carried out by a specialist teacher or psychologist that holds a specific qualification to conduct the assessment. This must be approved by the British Dyslexia Association.

Summative Assessment

Summative assessments happen at the end of a period of teaching. This could be at the end of a piece of work on a theme or unit at the end of a half term or term, or be a formal final examination such as Standardised Assessment Tests (SATS) or General Certificate of Secondary Education (GCSEs). We need to consider each of these summative assessment points for our neurodivergent pupils, as each one will hold challenges for them, and some may need access arrangements putting in to place. The following section will look at the assessment points as a timeline.

The Assessment Process: Summative Assessment Points

Table 5.1 has been adapted from Alix (2020) and outlines the different summative assessment points across the educational timeline.

Table 5.1 Pupil summative assessment stages and ages (Alix, 2020)

Age	Year group	Stage	Tests	Considerations
3–4		Preschool		Apply for primary school place
4–5	Reception	Foundation	Early Years Foundation Stage Profile	
5–6	Year 1	Key Stage 1	Phonics screening in which pupils demonstrate whether they are able to decode words for reading	Pupils are often tested throughout the year and at the end of every school year by whatever the individual school approach is
6–7	Year 2		National tests and tasks in numeracy and literacy – SATS	

(*Continued*)

Table 5.1 (Continued)

Age	Year group	Stage	Tests	Considerations
7–8 8–9 9–10 10–11	Year 3 Year 4 Year 5 Year 6	Key Stage 2	National tests and tasks in numeracy and literacy SATS, pupils aiming for a place at one of England's grammar schools may take the eleven plus exam	Apply for a secondary school place Pupils are often tested throughout the year and at the end of every school year by whatever the individual school approach is
11–12 12–13 13–14	Year 7 Year 8 Year 9	Key Stage 3	School internal tests, termly or annually	Choose options for years 10 and 11
14–15 15–16	Year 10 Year 11	Key Stage 4	Mock exams, GCSEs or other vocational qualifications	Apply for sixth form, college or apprenticeship Pupils are often tested throughout the year and at the end of every school year by whatever the individual school approach is
16–17 17–18	Year 12 Year 13 (if at sixth form)	Key Stage 5	Mock exams, A levels Post-16 qualifications Apprenticeships	Higher Education (HE) options and careers service
18+			Undergraduate certificates, diplomas, degrees, Higher National Certificate (HNC), Higher National Diploma (HND), work-based qualifications	Careers service

There are current Government expectations that all pupils will achieve at least five GCSE grades 4–9 which include Maths and English. Consider how these expectations may affect the self-esteem and well-being of neurodivergent pupils that are not on target to achieve these grades.

Case Study

From an LSA Working with a Child with ADHD

Jack found it difficult to concentrate, and there were too many distractions in the classroom. When it came to sitting tests and exams, Jack found it hard to stay focused, and with the additional stress from the expectations, he would feel low about his lack of achievement.

Often during class, he would take frequent breaks which would help him refocus for short periods of time. He also preferred to work in quieter areas of the school or class with less pupils in.

Using the assess, plan, do and review graduated approach, the SENCo and the class teacher had decided on some strategies to support Jack in class. The LSA was included in a meeting for Jack to discuss how these strategies could be put into place and what they would look like on a daily basis. These strategies included frequent planned breaks before Jack became restless, with the option to leave the classroom, and the consideration of how to support Jack with the approaching exams.

One focus was to work on Jack's self-esteem and well-being. He joined a group of other pupils for discussions around exam stress, expectations and moving forward from exams. I (as Jack's LSA) joined these groups so that I could follow up with Jack afterwards and remind him of the things discussed in the group when he was feeling low or frustrated when the work became too much for him. I liked the fact that I could join Jack for these groups rather than be sent elsewhere to work, as it meant that I could build my relationship with Jack further around his self-esteem and our relationship and trust developed.

The other focus was around the additional support that Jack may need for the exams.

Reflect

Do you work with any neurodivergent pupils with ADHD? How do they feel about exams and tests? Does the school offer any support groups for this or individual support? Are there any well-being or self-esteem programmes implemented within your school? If so, how would your pupils access these?

As we know from the GCSE expectations, expectations and pressure on pupils to do well in exams are high. Your neurodivergent pupils may work incredibly hard on their learning and make significant progress in many areas, but still not be at the national expectation levels. When supporting neurodivergent pupils such as this, it is important to find a balance recognising their effort and the progress that they make alongside recognising aspirations that everyone holds for them.

Schools assess against ARE, and some of your neurodivergent pupils with their neuro-learning differences will never be working at ARE, and instead will be 'working towards' them.

It is vital to consider the language that you use in front of your pupils; for example, celebrate the success in progress that has been made rather than saying a pupil has failed because they did not achieve ARE or the points needed to achieve national levels on a test or a grade 4 GCSE. When a pupil is working hard to make progress, it can be very demoralising and damaging to their well-being and self-esteem when grades and numbers are attached, or if they are compared to their peers.

Access Arrangements

Your neurodivergent pupils may need some adjustments made to exams and tests, and exam access arrangements can be applied for by the school SENCo.

These might be needed for any of your neurodivergent pupils and maybe because they have difficulty with reading, writing, processing, sensory processing and concentration, to name a few.

When the school applies for access arrangements, they will need to show that the pupil has a significant disadvantage to their peers if they did not have the requested adjustment. They also need to demonstrate that the pupil also already receives this adjustment as part of their normal classroom daily practice.

For example, when we look back at the case study with Jack, Jack had provision in place for him to take regular planned breaks and time out of the classroom, which leads to additional time for the work set. The SENCo could apply for the additional time for Jack and include planned breaks into his exam time.

The SENCo would apply for this additional time or for further adjustments such as:

- Time to open test papers early so that they can be copied onto coloured papers, diagrams and charts enlarged or enhanced, or for the preparing of equipment.
- The use of a scribe.
- The use of technological devices such as a laptop or word processor.
- The use of a reader.

Further reading on access arrangements and how the support can be used can be found in the 'Further Reading' section at the end of the chapter.

Case Study

Alaya was dyslexic and had difficulty with reading at pace and with spelling. During normal class time, she would have support through the use of additional resources including word banks, the use of classroom displays, additional time to complete work and pre-teaching of concepts and key language and terminology. As the exams approached, the teacher made use of the displays to put up key information for Alaya to refer to.

Adjustments were made for Alaya during the exams which included sitting the exams within the classroom rather than in the large hall. Display boards were covered, but being in the classroom supported Alaya in remembering key information. Alaya commented on feeling more relaxed being in her own classroom; she was also given an additional 25% more time allocation.

Professional Discussion

Discuss with your class teacher what provision might be available or applied for if you were working with a pupil like Alaya in your own class. Would they be able to take exams in a different room to the large hall? This might be beneficial for other neurodivergent pupils such as autistic pupils and pupils with sensory processing disorder or anxiety. What would be the benefits to each of these pupils?

There is the need to rethink and reform the approach to exams for our neurodivergent pupils. McPherson (2022) argues that we need to have a more inclusive approach and that our current system with an exam-based approach fails our neurodivergent pupils. He writes an article for the *Times Education Supplement (TES)* which is in the 'Further Reading' section at the end of the chapter, and it is a good place to read articles and debates on many educational topics that are current.

Strengths-Based Model

Neurodivergent pupils have many strengths, and they can easily get lost and hidden when focusing on areas to improve on. It is really important when using a neurodiversity model to focus on pupil strengths, to build on these and to ensure that there are opportunities to this. This should be included as part of the assessment process. Yes, looking for gaps in knowledge and skills will need to take place, but considering ways to build on pupil's strengths will provide development and opportunities as they move throughout their educational experiences and into their adult lives.

Armstrong (2012) is clear that neurodivergent pupils need to have positive role models that are neurodivergent themselves. Draw upon these to demonstrate to your pupils the achievements that everyone can have when they build upon their own strengths. Armstrong (2012: p. 146) presents a neurodiversity strengths checklist, which is a really useful tool to work through to identify key areas of strength and to celebrate these. The checklist covers area such as:

- Personal strengths; for example, keeps a personal diary or journal, has strong opinions about controversial topics, has good self-discipline, enjoys working independently.

- Communication strengths; for example, asks good questions, is a good storyteller, has good listening skills.
- Social strengths; for example, has at least one good friend, likes to play board games/card games with others, is polite and has good manners, follows class rules.
- Emotional strengths; for example, is emotionally sensitive to perceiving the world around them, has gut feelings about things.
- Cognitive strengths; for example, has good study skills, is able to pay close attention to detail, is able to become totally absorbed in an activity.
- Creative strengths; for example, enjoys doodling, drawing or painting; possesses a love of beautiful things; comes up with ideas that no one else has thought of.
- Literacy strengths; for example, enjoys reading books, enjoys listening to an audio book or someone telling a story.
- Logical strengths; for example, enjoys working with numbers, has an interest in astronomy, chemistry, physics or biology.
- Visio-spatial strengths; for example, is good at doing puzzles, gets information more easily through pictures rather than words.
- Physical strengths; for example, has a good sense of balance, likes to dance, is physically strong, has good flexibility.
- Dexterity strengths; for example, enjoys crafts, has good hand–eye coordination, has a hobby such as building model cars or other objects.
- Musical strengths; for example, enjoys listening to music, knows the lyrics and music of many songs, is sensitive to rhythms of music.
- Nature strengths; for example, has a good rapport with animas, is concerned about the welfare of the planet, enjoys studying nature.
- High-tech strengths; for example, likes to spend time on a computer, tablet or phone; enjoys playing video games; enjoys social media; likes using a camera or video to record events.
- Spiritual strengths; for example, enjoys meditation, asks big life questions, participates in religious or spiritual events.
- Cultural strengths; for example, is tolerant of others' differences; has pride in their own cultural, ethnic or racial background; enjoys learning about different cultural traditions.
- Other strengths; for example, likes collecting things, loves learning new things, manages money well, has good entrepreneurial skills.

(Armstrong, 2012)

As you can see, the list is vast and wide ranging. When you consider the content within these, you focus on the great range of strengths that your neurodivergent pupil has. Building in strengths to a pupil's IEP or EHCP can support pupil self-esteem and well-being, but often these documents focus on gaps that need to be filled and the negative aspects of what a pupil can't do yet. Ensure that you build your practice with pupils around a strengths-based approach and incorporate elements of this within your daily practice.

Chapter Summary

This chapter has given an overview of the main types of assessment in schools: assessment for learning, formative assessment and summative assessment. It has given an outline of the formal summative assessment points that happen within a pupil's education. We have considered how exams and tests and grading might impact on pupil self-esteem, well-being and anxiety, and this chapter can be cross-referenced with other chapters to seek further strategies for support for pupils demonstrating challenges and issues within these areas.

The chapter has looked at some of the different assessment tools that are used in schools and how these are not used as a diagnosis but as a tool to seek areas for development and supporting strategies that support staff might implement as part of their support and practice with pupils.

The graduated approach that is used has been outlined and the importance of this approach and how all staff contribute to feeding into the assess–plan–do–review cycle have been discussed. The chapter finishes with a look at the strengths-based model.

Glossary of Key Term

- The graduated approach – the cycle of assessment for SEND needs: assess–plan–do–review.

Further Reading

- Armstrong, T. (2012) *Neurodiversity in the Classroom; Strength-Based Strategies to Help Students with Special Needs Succeed in School and Life.* ASCD. Alexandria.
- Department for Education (2021) Key Stage 2 Access Arrangements Guidance. https://assets.publishing.service.gov.uk/government/uploads/system/uploads/attachment_data/file/1031081/2022_key_stage_2_access_arrangements_guidance.pdf.
- Glazzard, J. and Stones, S. (2021) *Evidence Based Primary Teaching.* SAGE. London.
- Glazzard, J. and Stones, S. (2021) *Evidence Based Secondary Teaching.* SAGE. London.
- McPherson, R. (2022). Neurodiversity: Why Exam Reform Is Urgent. www.tes.com/magazine/analysis/general/neurodiversity-why-exam-reform-urgentTES.
- National Association for Special Educational Needs (NASEN) (2022) Teacher Handbook: SEND; Embedding Inclusive Practice. Education

Endowment Foundation (EEF). www.wholeschoolsend.org.uk/resources/teacher-handbook-send.

- The Good Schools Guide (2022) Access Arrangements. www.good-schoolsguide.co.uk/special-educational-needs/your-rights/exam-access-arrangements.
- Watts, C. (2022) How to Use the Engagement Model in Schools. www.highspeedtraining.co.uk/hub/the-engagement-model-in-schools/.

References

Alix, S. (2020). *The Foster Carer's Handbook on Education; Getting the Best for Your Child*. CoramBAAF. London.

Armstrong, T. (2012). *Neurodiversity in the Classroom; Strength-Based Strategies to Help Students with Special Needs Succeed in School and Life*. ASCD. Alexandria.

Glazzard, J. and Stones, S. (2021a) *Evidence Based Primary Teaching*. SAGE. London.

Glazzard, J. and Stones, S. (2021b). *Evidence Based Secondary Teaching*. SAGE. London.

National Association for Special Educational Needs (NASEN) (2022). Teacher Handbook: SEND; Embedding Inclusive Practice (2022). Education Endowment Foundation (EEF). www.wholeschoolsend.org.uk/resources/teacher-handbook-send.

Watts, C. (2022). How to Use the Engagement Model in Schools. www.highspeedtraining.co.uk/hub/the-engagement-model-in-schools/.

Reflect

There are important links between assessment and the progress of pupils. Think back to Chapter 5, once you have carried out assessments: what strategies need to be implemented to support neurodivergent pupils to make progress? Consider the strategies coming up in Chapter 6 and how they work together with assessment.

6 Supporting Progression of Neurodivergent Pupils

Chapter Aims

- To gain an understanding of how educational learning theories such as the use of memory, metacognition, cognitive load and retrieval practice support neurodivergent learners in the classroom.
- To understanding the principles of Quality First Teaching (QFT) and how this is important for neurodivergent pupils.
- To gain an understanding of adaptive teaching.
- To examine the implementation of some general teaching strategies for neurodivergent pupils.
- To look at subject specific strategies for neurodivergent pupils.

Links to the Professional Standards for Teaching Assistants

Personal and Professional Conduct

- **5 Committing to improve their own practice** through self-evaluation and awareness.

Knowledge and Understanding

- **1 Acquire the appropriate skills, qualifications and/or experience** required for the teaching assistant role with support from the school employer.
- **2 Demonstrate expertise and skills in understanding the needs of all pupils** (including specialist expertise as appropriate) and know how to adapt and deliver support to meet individual needs.
- **3 Share responsibility for ensuring that their own knowledge and understanding is relevant and up to date** by reflecting on their own practice, liaising with school leaders and accessing relevant professional development to improve personal effectiveness.

DOI: 10.4324/9781003427599-7

- **4 Demonstrate a level of subject and curriculum knowledge relevant to their role** and apply this effectively in supporting teachers and pupils.

Teaching and Learning

- 1 Demonstrate an informed and efficient approach to teaching and learning by adopting relevant strategies to support the work of the teacher and increase achievement of all pupils including, where appropriate, those with special educational needs and disabilities.
- 4 Contribute to effective assessment and planning by supporting the monitoring, recording and reporting of pupil progress as appropriate to the level of the role.
- 5 Communicate effectively and sensitively with pupils to adapt to their needs and support their learning.
- 6 Maintain a stimulating and safe learning environment by organising and managing physical teaching space and resources.

Working with Others

- **1 Recognise and respect the role and contribution of other professionals, parents and carers** by liaising effectively and working in partnership with them.
- **2 With the class teacher, keep other professionals accurately informed** of progress or concerns they may have about the pupils they work with.
- **3 Understand their responsibility to share knowledge** to inform planning and decision-making.
- **4 Understand their role** in order to be able to work collaboratively with classroom teachers and other colleagues, including specialist advisory teachers.
- **5 Communicate their knowledge and understanding of pupils** to other school staff and education, health and social care professionals so that informed decision-making can take place on intervention and provision.

Introduction

This chapter provides information on specific teaching and learning strategies that you as teaching assistants (TAs) and learning support assistants (LSAs) will be able to use to support neurodivergent pupils. There are many new learning theories and learning sciences that are being implemented and embedded within schools, and depending upon how current your school is with their training in this area, will depend on what experience you may already have.

This chapter will cover some of the key learning theories and why they are important to use with your pupils with neuro-learning differences.

Some of the strategies discussed should be used with all pupils such as QFT, High Quality Teaching (HQT) and adaptive teaching, and each is particularly useful with neurodivergent pupils.

Learning Theories and Sciences

New and current learning theories are very much a part of schools today. Sometimes they are referred to as 'learning sciences' in relation to more traditional learning theories that you may have read about. The learning theories and sciences that are current are rooted in evidence-based practice (another term used a great deal in schools and educational practice). These research-informed theories are heavily endorsed by the Department for Education and by Ofsted.

The Education Endowment Foundation (EEF) which writes and researches extensively within education does acknowledge though that these learning sciences may not work for all pupils and that some of the implementation of the theories may not be applied effectively and therefore become lost within the practice. Therefore, it is really important to read further around the theories to gain a better understanding of how to implement them with your neurodivergent pupils so that they become a part of your daily practice.

Memory

There are three main types of memory that we use all of the time: sensory memory, working memory and long-term memory. You may be more familiar with the second and third, working memory and long-term memory, which is where most educational reading will focus, but the first, sensory memory, is less heard of, but it is incredibly important and even more so with our neurodivergent pupils.

First, for example, we see, hear, smell, taste or touch something (sensory), which is then drawn into our working memory as we decide whether it is worth taking note of and committing our attention to it. As it works through working memory, parts of that information are stored into our long-term memory.

When the sensory memory is activated, neurotypical learners will be able to filter out the information that they do not need to pay attention to, for example, a dripping tap, a ticking clock, the chatter of other pupils' voices or bright and colourful wall displays, but for neurodivergent pupils, this type of stimuli becomes a distraction and they cannot filter it out easily. Therefore, working memory is disrupted due to the oversensitivity of the sensory memory, with some neurodivergent pupils overloading their working memory with sensory overload.

Once we have decided which stimuli to focus on, this then becomes part of our working memory. Then information which we want to hold on to is moved into long-term memory. Some of this is encoded, and some of this is lost. Retrieval practice is very important in strengthening recall from the long-term memory so that we can use it again and again. Over time, recall becomes easier, and the information becomes more easily accessible from our long-term memory if we recall it regularly. Therefore, teaching practices and strategies such as retrieval practice and spaced learning (which we will look at in this chapter) are important to incorporate.

The EEF's (2021) *Cognitive Science Approaches in the Classroom: A Review of the Evidence* is a useful document which outlines effective learning theory approaches and strategies to use in the classroom, which are supported by evidence-based research.

Let's look at some of these now.

Metacognition and Self-Regulated Learning

When pupils think about their own learning, where they are at, what they are doing and the choices that they make, this is metacognition – thinking about thinking. The EEF (2018) states that when the use of metacognition in the classroom is introduced and implemented effectively, then it can make as much as seven months' progress on pupils learning.

The monitoring, control and direction of learning by learners is metacognition as defined by Muijs and Bokhove (2020). They state that when a learner has knowledge of monitoring their own learning, monitoring whether strategies work for them, adapting them and using them again (e.g. when using feedback or redrafting work), checking success criteria in a lesson, deciding what has gone well for them in a piece of work or whether they have needed to overcome any difficulties, then this is metacognition.

Muijs and Bokhove (2020) define that self-regulated learning includes all of this but with cognition and the consideration of the extent to which a learner understands their strengths and areas for development.

Both metacognition and self-regulated learning are clearly interlinked, and some researchers believe that metacognition is a part of self-regulated learning, and others believe it is the opposite way around. Research is still developing in this area, and concepts will become clearer when there are further examples of it being used in class. Either way, supporting neurodivergent learners to take ownership of their learning to support their own progress and to increase their self-esteem in knowing how to develop and adapt strategies to support their own learning is very beneficial to them.

Sherrington and Caviglioli (2022: p. 36) have written a set of books named *walkthrus*. These give step-by-step guides to core teaching strategies that you can use to understand the process and how to implement a particular strategy. This particular text outlines metacognition and self-regulation in five steps:

1 Explicitly teach how to plan, monitor and evaluate.
2 Model your own thinking.
3 Set an appropriate level of challenge.
4 Promote and develop metacognitive talk.
5 Explicitly teach how to organise and manage learning.

They are incredibly useful books to retain and to use as your own guide for implementing strategies with your pupils. Links to these books are in the 'Further Reading' section of this chapter.

Glazzard and Stones (2021a, b) support the model of metacognition focusing on a cycle for the learner:

• Setting goals.
• Planning how to achieve them.
• Monitoring progress towards goals.
• Evaluating whether goals have been achieved.
• Reflecting on the next steps.
• Returning to setting goals.

You will need to consider adding in levels of deliberate difficulty to ensure that pupils have some cognitive demand on them and that the cognitive load is at the right level for their existing frameworks and knowledge that they already hold. Scaffolding such as adult support and the use of resources such as manipulatives or writing frames can be put into place, and then slowly removed to develop their independence.

Cognitive Load Theory

Cognitive load theory centres around the use of working memory. Working memory can be overloaded, and I am sure that we can all think of times when we are trying to hold too much information and we forget things. This is because working memory has a limited capacity, and when it becomes full, information will be lost. The Centre for Education Statistics and Evaluation (2017) discusses the theory of cognitive load. It outlines three types:

• Intrinsic load – in which if the complexity of the information being given is too high, and the underlying knowledge base of the learner has not reached this level yet, then the cognitive load for the learner is too much and the information will not be understood or retained. This has a negative impact on the learner.
• Extraneous load – this is when the learner is asked to solve a problem, but they do not yet have the skills or the process to do this. The learner tries to solve the problem, rather than using a technique that will help them to do this (think of maths problems and using formulae) because they do not have the formula. This will also have a negative impact on the learner.

- Germane load – this is when instruction is given to support the development of schema to then help learner progress. The instruction gives examples of how to work out the problem and how it can be replicated when the learner is given a similar problem to solve. This will have a positive impact on learning.

Intrinsic and extraneous loads can have a detrimental effect on neurodivergent learners for both their learning and their self-esteem when they find work overwhelming when they do not have the knowledge or skills to draw upon to carry out the task that has been given. This could potentially lead to negative behaviours being exhibited.

Reflect

Think of an example of practice that you have seen for each of the three types of cognitive load: intrinsic, extraneous and germane.

Now think of an example when you have potentially used each of these three types of load with one of your neurodivergent learners. What were the outcomes for them? What will you need to consider and do differently next time?

Unpacking cognitive load is really important, and you need to recognise when this is happening, and how you need to change what you are doing to scaffold your neurodivergent learner.

Retrieval Practice

Retrieval practice can be seen in many lessons and is one of the more common learning sciences that are understood and used by teachers. It is where the information is retrieved from long-term memory so that it is reinforced and is easier to retrieve the more that it is recalled. Retrieval practice is seen in the classroom through the use of quizzes and what is classed as low-stakes questions or tests, in which pupils can retrieve the information without having the stress of formal exams or tests. It is often carried out in a fun and engaging way. It is good for self-esteem, and when carried out in a safe environment, it demonstrates that it is ok to make mistakes, or not know something.

Spaced Practice

Spaced practice is when the teaching of concepts is taught over a prolonged period of time. For example, the content is chunked into sections and spaced out over a half term or term. It is often used alongside retrieval practice and with content revisited back and forth.

Reflect

Think about your teaching with an individual pupil over the last week. Did you use any of the above methods? What did it look like? Could you improve on how you have implemented them? If you have not used retrieval practice before, how could you have adapted one of your teaching sessions in the past week to include retrieval practice? Would this have been beneficial to your pupil? Why?

Quality First Teaching

QFT was introduced in 2010, and has been changed and adapted over the years. High Quality Teaching (HQT) is now also referred to in various educational documents. The core principles of QFT remain. HQT is delivered to all pupils through teaching methods that are proven through evidence-based research to work. QFT is the starting block for all types of teaching regardless of whether pupils have special educational needs and disabilities or are neurodivergent. This approach incorporates adaptive teaching, which is discussed in the next section, and scaffolding learners to achieve outcomes.

Previously there was a model in place called the 'wave model', and some staff may still refer to this. The wave model had three tiers: the first was the universal tier, which outlined QFT. The second tier was for additional interventions and included guided work or small group teaching and activities. The third tier included specialised interventions for pupils where more personalisation was needed. Tiers two and three were additional to tier one and not instead of them.

Some schools will still use the language of waves or tiers, and others have introduced their own explanations to outline the differences such as core, enhanced and bespoke, or universal, targeted and specialist. Is there specific terminology that your school uses or within your Local Authority?

QFT strategies include:

- Securing **subject knowledge** of the person delivering the lesson or teaching. Teachers and LSAs/TA may need further Continuing Professional Development (CPD) to develop their subject knowledge in specific areas to ensure that they are secure in delivering the content of the subjects taught. This will include having the knowledge of the best teaching methods and strategies and the resources to teach the subject.
- Making **explicit links** between prior knowledge and teaching to the new knowledge being taught. This will support recall of methods, strategies and knowledge that pupils will need to draw upon for that particular session.
- The use of **small step planning** to support cognitive load (as discussed earlier) and working memory so that pupils do not have to cope with too much information, or information that they do not have the skills to work with. The use of chunking is useful here.

- **Planning for misconceptions** and errors that pupils may make. Antici-pating problems will help teachers and LSAs/TAs be prepared to support pupils and recognise what may need to be changed.
- Using **manipulatives and resources** to support pupils through scaffold-ing learning and pupil understanding. Scaffolds can be removed as pupils develop their skills and confidence.
- Using **metacognition** by the teacher, LSA or TA when explaining or modelling will show pupils your own thinking process that you are going through and the choices you have made. Talk partners is also useful here so that pupils can practise talking about their thinking and choices and be able to talk this through with their partner.
- Teaching explicitly **new vocabulary** and giving examples of how and when it might be used.
- Using **deliberate practice** through breaking down concepts and skills and opportunities to practise these over and over again so that they are em-bedded and pupils are secure in this. This can then be supported through retrieval practice.

Reflect

Look at each of the elements above, and reflect back on a lesson from last week: when did you see each of these elements being used? How were they being used? If you have a lesson plan from the lesson, high-light each of these areas so that you can develop your recognition of them. Do you use these when you are teaching your neurodivergent pupils in groups or one to one? Do you use all of them or some of them? Are you more confident with particular areas of QFT and need to de-velop other areas?

If you were observing a lesson and looking for QFT, the elements that you would expect to see are:

- A focused learning outline for the lesson.
- Pupils involved and engaged with their learning.
- The use of appropriate questioning, modelling and explanation from the teacher.
- Pupils learning through talking with each other and the teacher.
- Pupils taking ownership and responsibility for their learning.
- Pupils using praise and encouragement are being used.

Look out for each of these when you are next supporting a lesson, and think how you might take these elements in to your own group and individual work.

Adaptive Teaching

Schools have now moved away from 'differentiation' in that all work was differentiated for different abilities of pupils. This may include different worksheets, tasks or objectives for pupils.

Firstly, think of 'attainment' rather 'ability'. Attainment is the level in which a pupil is currently working at, rather than ability is capping what a pupil can do in that area. When we talk about different groups, refer to attainment rather than ability, for example, higher attainers or lower attainers. This shows that they are working at a particular level at this moment in time, this is what they are achieving or attaining, but as we know with our neurodivergent learners, there can be many barriers in the way to what a pupil could potentially achieve, and this is not based upon their ability to do so.

Differentiation may form as part of adaptive teaching, but again, teaching has moved on from just using differentiation as a method. Differentiation used in the way it had previously been used could cap pupil achievement due to the restriction being placed on pupils through the work being given.

Adaptive teaching takes a different approach in which all pupils are working towards the same objective and using scaffolding and supports for pupils to achieve the same objective. Scaffolds and supports can then be removed as pupils increase their skills, knowledge and confidence in the area.

Reflect

Think about applying adaptive teaching approaches with one of your neurodivergent pupils. You will have a good understanding of your pupil, and you will have knowledge of the barriers that they individually face when trying to learn; it could be to do with processing, reading, sensory, communication or relationships with their peers. How might this affect their learning within a particular lesson?

What scaffolds might you need to put in place for them? It could be the use of manipulatives or resources, or it could be facilitating and supporting paired or group work.

It is important to monitor and assess pupil progress when you are using scaffolding, and you will need to report this back to your class teacher as part of the graduated approach seen in Chapter 5.

Consider how the pupil has tackled the task: have they worked independently? Did they use resources? For how long? Did they complete the work? Did you need to adjust the scaffolding and offer additional support? Will the plans need adjusting for this pupil for the following day?

Scaffolding is useful to support working memory, cognitive load, filtering out distractions, changing tasks, organisation, reviewing and redrafting work and managing emotions.

Modelling

An important aspect of scaffolding is the use of modelling. It is a key part to any lesson by a teacher, and you will use this repeatedly with your pupils if needed, so ensure that you understand the method being used. Repeating the modelling or using different examples will support your neurodivergent pupils to embed the knowledge and skills from working memory to long-term memory.

Sherrington and Caviglioli (2020) outline explaining and modelling in their *walkthrus* book. As mentioned previously, these are a fantastic resource to take you through step by step each way of working with pupils. They are an essential part of your reading and learning toolkit as a member of staff working with pupils.

The Importance of Language

Difficulties with language processing and communication are common within the neurodiverse community. School has many forms of communication and therefore adds further difficulties and barriers. Let's look at three common types of communication in school: written, verbal and visual.

Written

Difficulties in writing can begin very early on within a pupil's education. Holding a pencil in the correct way, sitting in a correct writing position and understanding the school handwriting style are all difficulties neurodivergent pupils may face before they have even begun the writing process itself.

Your pupils may need pencil grips, cushions or footrests to support their writing position, and some pupils may find this physically uncomfortable for them, particularly pupils with sensory challenges or attention-deficit hyperactivity disorder. If you think that your pupil may be having difficulties in these areas, seek further advice and discussion from your class teacher and Special Educational Needs Co-ordinator (SENCo) and see if there are any resources that might help with these. As a member of support staff, you are more likely to be working with pupils during the writing process and will see these difficulties more often than other members of staff.

The complexity of the writing process continues with letter formation, spelling, punctuation, grammar, the creation and development of ideas and presenting work in so many different ways: stories, reports and experiments, to name a few. These are all areas in which modelling and scaffolding are greatly needed, and further strategies are discussed in the upcoming sections.

Verbal

The area of verbal communication has previously been discussed in Chapter 3.

Visual

Visual forms of communication include a wide range of communication methods within schools: signs, symbols, body language and facial expressions. As we know, some of these forms of visual communication could be beneficial for our neurodivergent pupils such as the use of signs and symbols, but the use of body language and facial expressions could be challenging and form a barrier.

Signs and symbols can be used to support communication in the form of outlining timetables for pupils, setting out what is to be completed during the day. They can support written or verbal communication in ways in which our neurodivergent pupils can potentially access more easily or quickly. However, other forms of visual communications such as the use of posters or displays may be too 'noisy' for neurodivergent pupils and have too much information on with colour, pictures and charts, and it may be difficult for pupils to pick out the information that they need to access, for example, posters on after school clubs or school trips.

General Strategies

Additional general supportive strategies for each of the core subject areas are outlined below. Make a note of those that you already do with your pupils, ones that you could improve on using and ones that you don't use, but will begin to put into your practice.

Reading

Many neurodivergent pupils have difficulties with reading for different reasons. Your school will have particular strategies or interventions in place that they may like you to use, and this section provides some general strategies that will support your pupils.

- Read written instructions out loud to pupils first.
- Ensure that you give pupils enough time to read and process the information given.
- Present materials clearly and without clutter so that pupils can access the information that they need.

- Discuss the meanings of words, and check that pupils understand them and provide context for them.
- Encourage pupils to highlight words that are key important pieces of information for them to use; they can write notes or doodles next to them.
- Consider the use of software such as text reading pens.

Writing

There are different reasons for pupils having difficulty with writing. It could be the physical aspect of writing, and it could be processing information that is needed before writing or generating ideas to begin the writing process. Some strategies that could support your neurodivergent pupils with some of these aspects are:

- Ensure that your pupil has a pen or pencil grip if needed.
- Allow time for pupils to talk through ideas first or to practise their sentences.
- Provide sentence starters to scaffold pupils in beginning their work.
- Ensure that you have provided enough time for pupils to complete a written task.
- Use a scribe to capture the ideas and sentences from a pupil.
- Give time for pupils to proofread work and make any changes that they would like to.
- Consider the use of a computer, scribe or voice note to record work in a different way to writing.

Maths

Some neurodivergent pupils may have specific difficulties with maths such as dyscalculia. This can also be seen across a range of other curriculum subjects in which maths is commonly used such as within science. Strategies to support some of these areas include:

- Practising using calendars and diaries.
- Using timelines of event.
- Using timetables for travel
- Using timers for tasks
- Using a range of concrete mathematical equipment both in maths and in other subjects when needed
- Explaining the use of equipment clearly

Independence and Organisation (Executive Functioning)

Some neurodivergent pupils will have a neuro-difference in organisation, preparing and planning. They have challenges in these areas that do not fit a neurotypical view of how to do things and the expectations held around these areas to deal with school and everyday life. This area of difficulty is known as difficulty with executive functioning.

Within school, the challenges may be seen through the pupil not having the right equipment for the lesson, or they arrive at the wrong classroom at the wrong time. This is because their 'executive function' does not work in the same way as your neurotypical pupils and neurodivergent pupils may find it overwhelming to cope with these elements on their own. This is an area that neurodivergent pupils may find challenging throughout their lives, so preparing them with access to supporting strategies that will be useful for them to take forward into adulthood is beneficial to them.

Some strategies to support executive function could include:

- Equipment lists for each lesson printed on the inside of their book or as a booklet.
- Timetables which include a visual element.
- Tasks broken down into small chunks.
- Time to check preparation against plans.
- Lists that can be checked off when something is complete.
- The use of alarms or reminders when something needs to be done.
- The use of organisational apps as reminders and timers (e.g. Brain in Hand, Timmo).

Pre-teaching

Pre-teaching is an important strategy for supporting neurodivergent pupils. As an LSA or TA, it may be included as part of your role to pre-teach groups or individuals around a concept or new vocabulary that will be introduced within the main lesson.

Pre-teaching supports pupils in being given additional time to process and understand new material prior to the lesson, which, in turn, supports their confidence and engagement within the lesson. It can also have a positive effect on a pupil's behaviour if a pupil normally feels frustrated by not understanding something.

Your teacher will identify the gaps in pupil knowledge or where a pupil would benefit from being introduced to new learning prior to the main lesson. It could be in relation to a specific task, skill, new knowledge or vocabulary. You would then introduce this to them either within a small group or individually. It might be outside the classroom or within the classroom if other pupils are working on something else. You would use the cognitive sciences through your explanation, visual and concrete supports and examples.

Read the case study below and consider how this example of pre-teaching may apply to you in your context, with your pupils, in your year groups.

Case Study

An LSA Supporting a Design and Technology Lesson

The class teacher was finding it difficult to work with Leon during Design and Technology (D&T) lessons. Leon was diagnosed as autistic and dyslexic. The teacher had noticed that Leon lacked the skills needed to use the equipment during the lessons, and he lacked confidence, which then led to Leon becoming disruptive so that he would leave the classroom.

Firstly, the teacher looked at Leon's Individual Education Plan (IEP) to check he hadn't missed anything that might be related to fine motor skills or using specific tools. Although the IEP didn't have anything specific on this, it was noted that Leon sometimes had difficulty grasping new concepts. The teacher also reflected upon how Leon would often hang back from getting involved in activities and prefer other pupils to do the work.

The teacher also spoke with the SENCo and discussed how Leon didn't particularly like noise and movement around the classroom, and that this could also be having an impact as D&T was an active lesson with pupils moving around to use equipment and lots of discussion during this time. Leon could therefore be withdrawing from this active part of the lesson to avoid it.

The teacher spoke with Tina the LSA to discuss some of their ideas for support that could benefit Leon and it was decided:

- Tina would pre-teach Leon some of the techniques that he would need for the lesson. They would do this during tutor reading time. Leon would spend some time one to one with Tina modelling the use of the equipment, and then he was practicing using a chunking method of each stage of the use of the equipment.
- Ensure that Leon was sitting in a quieter part of the classroom away from movement during the times when he did not need to use the fixed equipment that was set up in a particular area of the classroom.
- For Leon to work in a pair rather than within a group.

Activity

Take a lesson plan from a recent lesson taught by one of your teachers (any subject) in which you support a neurodivergent pupil.

Consider the pupil Leon in the previous case study. If Leon was having similar difficulties in this subject in this lesson (from your lesson plan), what adjustments could be made and what pre-teaching might be beneficial for him?

Specific Subject Areas

Additional consideration might be needed for your neurodivergent pupils within particular subject areas than those already seen or can be transferred from core subjects. The next section will consider some of these specific strategies for you to try.

Art

There can often be less structure to lesson time during art, or there may be more movement around a classroom, or pupils may have difficulty generating ideas for pieces of work or projects. Some pupils with sensory challenges may have difficulties working with the textures of some of the materials. Consider moving pupils to a quieter area of the classroom or creating a quieter area with less movement, and consider how you will draw upon strategies that you have already seen or read about to support neurodivergent pupils with generating ideas, and planning and preparation before committing them to paper for practical pieces of work.

Design and Technology

In addition to the example given in the case study with Leon, some pupils may have difficulties around anxiety and the use of equipment. In particular within cooking, the use of sharp knives or a hot cooker, or the use of large machinery in wood or metal work may cause your neurodivergent pupil to avoid wanting to join in with the lesson. Pre-teaching can be really beneficial in these cases where a pupil can practice in a quieter and safer environment as seen within the case study.

Drama

Pupils may have difficulty with inference when analysing texts; they may find decoding words, comprehension of the text and then inferring characters' thoughts and feelings very difficult. Drama can be beneficial in these circumstances, as it gives pupils the opportunity to explore characters and to see other pupils explore characters through role-play and hot-seating. However, some pupils may feel anxious about doing this; they may need further scaffolding through paired work, modelling, the use of speaking frames, sentence structures, word banks and key vocabulary.

Music

Neurodivergent pupils with sensory difficulties can find music challenging. Some pupils may not be able to attend music lessons as they find them too difficult to cope with the noises being made from a range of instruments and other pupils all playing different things at different times. You could consider some time for a pupil to explore an instrument and the sounds it makes prior to a lesson. Some pupils may benefit from using ear defenders so that they can still join in the lesson, but block out the louder noises when needed, or see if there is an adjoining classroom where a pupil can work that would be quieter.

Physical Education (PE)

As we have noted in Chapter 2, neurodivergent pupils can experience difficulties associated with the many complexities of PE before the lesson such as the changing area, getting changed for the lesson and time taken to change.

Furthermore, some pupils, particularly autistic pupils, can be very rule bound, sticking to rules rigidly which can impact on behaviour through confrontation and disagreements over the rules of games, cheating and group work. It is important that your neurodivergent pupil feels heard, rules are explained clearly and you unpick any challenges that may have arisen.

Science

Within science, consider the use of equipment as we have for other lessons such as D&T. You will also need to consider sensory challenges such as strong smells or loud noises that could occur during an experiment.

A scribe, a voice recorder, word banks and pre-teaching key vocabulary are all useful strategies to support science lessons.

Chapter Summary

This chapter has focused upon strategies to support the progress of your neurodivergent learners. You have been introduced to learning theories and sciences and how they are used in the classroom. Ensure that you take the time to understand these and take up training on these to embed them into your own practice. You have considered QFT, which aspect of this you see in class and which aspects you are already using yourself and what you need to improve on. You have also considered adaptive teaching and how you will include modelling and scaffolding into your practice with your neurodivergent learners.

You have also begun to think how strategies can be used across subjects and which subjects need further thought around the potential challenges that your neurodivergent learners may face.

Glossary of Key Terms

- Ability – the potential of a person to do something.
- Adaptive teaching – using adaptive teaching approaches to scaffold learners.
- Attainment – achievement at the current time.

- Cognitive Load Theory – when working memory is overloaded, information is not transferred effectively to long-term memory.
- Executive Function – a set of cognitive skills that include working memory, flexible thinking and self-control. These skills are used every day to learn, work and manage daily life. Neurodivergent pupils with executive function challenges can make it hard to focus, follow directions and handle emotions.
- Metacognition – the process of thinking about learning.
- Pre-teaching – a teaching strategy that is used to pre-teach new vocabulary or concepts to pupils.
- Quality First Teaching (QFT) – a teaching strategy where teaching methods are used to deliver high-quality teaching for all pupils.
- Retrieval practice – when information is retrieved from long-term memory through the use of quizzes, questions and tests.

Further Reading

- Education Endowment Foundation (2018) Metacognition and Self-Regulated Learning. https://educationendowmentfoundation.org.uk/education-evidence/guidance-reports/metacognition.
- Education Endowment Foundation (2021) Cognitive Science Approaches in the Classroom: A Review of the Evidence.
- Glazzard, J. and Stones, S. (2021) *Evidence Based Primary Teaching*. SAGE. London.
- Glazzard, J. and Stones, S. (2021) *Evidence Based Secondary Teaching*. SAGE. London.
- National Association for Special Educational Needs (NASEN) (2022) Teacher Handbook: SEND; Embedding Inclusive Practice. Education Endowment Foundation (EEF). https://www.wholeschoolsend.org.uk/resources/teacher-handbook-send.
- Sherrington, T. and Caviglioli, O. (2020) *Teaching Walkthrus*. John Catt Publishing. Woodbridge.
- Sherrington, T. and Caviglioli, O. (2022) *Teaching Walkthrus 3*. John Catt Publishing. Woodbridge.
- The Centre for Education Statistics and Evaluation (2017) Cognitive Load Theory: Research That Teachers Really Need to Understand. NSW Department of Education.

References

Glazzard, J. and Stones, S. (2021a) *Evidence Based Primary Teaching*. SAGE. London.
Glazzard, J. and Stones, S. (2021b) *Evidence Based Secondary Teaching*. SAGE. London.

Muijs, D. and Bokhove, C. (2020) *Metacognition and Self-Regulation: Evidence Review*. Education Endowment Foundation. London.

Sherrington, T. and Caviglioli, O. (2022) *Teaching Walkthrus 3*. John Catt Publishing. Woodbridge.

The Centre for Education Statistics and Evaluation (2017) Cognitive Load Theory: Research that Teachers Really Need to Understand. NSW Department of Education.

Reflect

Think about Quality First Teaching: when do you see this taking place in your classroom? Identify what this looks like, and then consider how you have contributed to implementing this as a learning support assistant/ teaching assistant last week in your own teaching with neurodivergent pupils.

7   Working in Different Formats
One-to-One, Groups and Interventions

Chapter Aims

- To develop practice in working on a one-to-one basis with neurodivergent pupils.
- To develop practice in working with groups of neurodivergent pupils.
- To develop practice when working with interventions and neurodivergent pupils.

Links to the Professional Standards for Teaching Assistants

- **5 Committing to improve their own practice** through self-evaluation and awareness.

Knowledge and Understanding

- **1 Acquire the appropriate skills, qualifications and/or experience** required for the teaching assistant role with support from the school employer.
- **2 Demonstrate expertise and skills in understanding the needs of all pupils** (including specialist expertise as appropriate) and know how to adapt and deliver support to meet individual needs.
- **3 Share responsibility for ensuring that their own knowledge and understanding is relevant and up to date** by reflecting on their own practice, liaising with school leaders and accessing relevant professional development to improve personal effectiveness.
- **4 Demonstrate a level of subject and curriculum knowledge relevant to their role** and apply this effectively in supporting teachers and pupils.

DOI: 10.4324/9781003427599-8

Teaching and Learning

- 1 Demonstrate an informed and efficient approach to teaching and learning by adopting relevant strategies to support the work of the teacher and increase achievement of all pupils including, where appropriate, those with special educational needs and disabilities.
- 2 Promote, support and facilitate inclusion by encouraging participation of all pupils in learning and extracurricular activities.
- 3 Use effective behaviour management strategies consistently in line with the school's policy and procedures.
- 4 Contribute to effective assessment and planning by supporting the monitoring, recording and reporting of pupil progress as appropriate to the level of the role.
- 5 Communicate effectively and sensitively with pupils to adapt to their needs and support their learning.
- 6 Maintain a stimulating and safe learning environment by organising and managing physical teaching space and resources.

Working with Others

- **2 With the class teacher, keep other professionals accurately informed** of progress or concerns they may have about the pupils they work with.
- **3 Understand their responsibility to share knowledge** to inform planning and decision-making.
- **4 Understand their role** in order to be able to work collaboratively with classroom teachers and other colleagues, including specialist advisory teachers.
- **5 Communicate their knowledge and understanding of pupils** to other school staff and education, health and social care professionals, so that informed decision-making can take place on intervention and provision.

Introduction

A great deal of your work as a teaching assistant (TA) or learning support assistant (LSA) will be working with neurodivergent pupils on a one-to-one basis or working with small groups within classes or implementing specialist-focussed interventions. This chapter will look at each of these three areas and will give you the opportunity to reflect on how this type of work is developing and whether specific strategies can be implemented to improve this area of work for your own practice.

Working with Pupils on a One-to-One Basis

As a TA or LSA you may have all of your time allocated to working with one specific pupil on a one-to-one basis. Or you may work with a pupil, but also within a group or a whole class setting, or you may need to give a pupil additional support at particular periods throughout the day.

As you will now know from the Education Endowment Foundation (EEF; 2018) document, working directly with a pupil on a one-to-one basis, 100% of the time is not good practice (re-read this now; the link is in the 'Further Reading' section of this chapter). It can lead to challenges such as the pupil becoming reliant upon one person, they have expectations of support at all times and it can prevent them from building up independent working and resilience. Some parents or carers may have an expectation that their child should have a one-to-one person working with them at all times, and this perception should be discussed with the parent or carer by the class teacher or Special Educational Needs Co-ordinator (SENCo) so that they understand what is happening in the classroom, and why it is happening; this can prevent any ongoing challenges and confrontations by the parents through clarity of expectations and understanding of what best practice in schools looks like.

So, what might be your role if you are working with a pupil on a one-to-one basis?

There are several strategies that you may need to use, whether you are working with a pupil in every lesson or with them through part of the day.

- You may need to check in on the child and set out the expectations and timetable for the day, ensuring that your pupil understands what is to follow throughout the day and what lessons will be taking place.
- You may need to support facilitation of the unstructured times of the day such as the transition times between lessons, and break times and lunch times.
- You may need to give hover support when a pupil is working on a task in class – checking in with them, looking over what they are doing and where they are at, and offering encouragement and praise to keep them on track or motivated. You are working towards independence, so the balance of this may change from lesson to lesson and over time.
- Your hover support may include some taught elements when needed.
- Ensure that you know the pupil's Individual Education Plan (IEP) or Education, Health and Care Plan (EHCP) targets, and that you understand what you are doing with them to support them, is working towards these targets.
- Get to know your pupil's family: what is working for them? Is there anything that you should know so that you can support your pupil further?
- Ensure that you feed back regularly to your class teacher. Your pupil is their responsibility, and good communication between yourself and the class teacher is vital so that informed decisions can be made around reviewing their progress and adjusting the provision that they are receiving.

Reflect

Which of the above strategies do you already implement? Are there any areas which are more difficult such as providing hover support? If so, what will be your next steps in discussing this with your class teacher or line manager to move your practice forward and the learning for your pupils?

Working with Groups of Neurodivergent Pupils

Working with groups of neurodivergent pupils can be particularly challenging for both the TA/LSA working with them and the neurodivergent pupils. Neurodivergent pupils can find group work challenging for a range of reasons: communication and language issues, anxiety and sensory needs.

Some pupils could have language and comprehension barriers, not understanding phrases being used, or jokes that are made by others in the group can cause confusion and distress. Pupils may have difficulty in expressing their ideas or their thoughts through the use of language and due to the anxiety that this may cause; they could lack engagement within the group or not have their say in activities. Some neurodivergent pupils may have difficulty with the construction and process of a conversation, for example, turn taking, listening, waiting, pausing for breath, using facial expressions and being polite.

Other pupils may prefer to work on their own. Pupils who have a strong sense of rules may want to work within their own boundaries and frameworks and not contribute to group activities, or not take on the ideas of other pupils towards work that they will need to call their own. They may also become upset if other pupils in the group do not stay on task or follow the instructions that are given.

To start with, create group rules or an agreement of expected behaviours for the group. This will provide some boundaries and safety points to refer back to when needed. Rules could include:

- Take turns.
- Listen when someone else is speaking.
- Be respectful of other pupils' ideas.
- Encourage and support other pupils to contribute and join in.
- Take responsibility for a role within a task.
- If you want to disagree, disagree politely and give a reason why you disagree.
- Listen to feedback and act upon it.

When carrying out group work, consider where pupils are sitting. Although you might not be able to control who is in the group, you can think about the pupils within the group and which pupils might work better with each other. Think about their strengths and challenges, and the type of task or activity that you might be doing: are there any pupils that will be better taking a lead role or encouraging other pupils to join in? Or are there pupils within your group that are stronger with their reading skills or discussing ideas? You may want pupils to work in pairs within the group rather than all pupils contributing to the discussion or task. You will still be able to listen and support each of the pairs within the group.

After group work, take the time to reflect on how it went, what worked well and what needs to be worked on to improve the group working. Think about the individual pupils' participation within the group and what you might change next time to improve this.

If you are finding that some of your neurodivergent pupils are struggling with group work, think about the purpose of the task. Is it important that they carry out the work in this way? What is the aim of the work? Could they carry out the work independently? What are the objectives for the lesson?

You also need to consider whether your pupils are working on targets on an IEP or EHCP. These may include targets around group work, working with others or communication and language skills. These may need to be taken into consideration alongside the tasks and the lesson objectives. You may be working on two sets of objectives and need to decide which objective needs to take priority. From this, you then need to feedback to your class teacher and discuss any issues and challenges surrounding this.

Working in Pairs

Working in pairs can help to develop skills in preparation for group work and has many benefits. One idea to support this development that you may have already seen being used in class is think–pair–share, or you may have used this yourself with pupils.

Think–pair–share is a strategy that is designed to encourage student involvement. First, participants listen to the teacher's question. Then they think of a response. They pair up with someone and discuss their responses. Finally, they are asked to share their responses with the whole group. This can be implemented within your small group working.

Think–pair–share is usually referred to as a Kagan structure, but it was developed originally by Frank Lyman and Arlene Mindus in 1977 and adapted as part of the Kagan structures.

Kagan structures promote four major principles, following the acronym PIES:

- Positive independence.
- Individual accountability.
- Equal participation.
- Simultaneous interaction.

You can see from the above principles how this may support pupil engagement and pupils' taking responsibility for their own learning as outlined in Chapters 5 and 6. There are some links in the 'Further Reading' section of this chapter for you to explore Kagan strategies further.

Case Study

From the Perspective of an LSA

Zaria worked as an LSA with year 6. She often worked with groups of pupils but found it more challenging when one of her pupils, Mushana, was in the group. Mushana had a diagnosis of autism and dyslexia. When Mushana was in the group, the group always ended up having arguments and Mushana became agitated and distressed, moving around the classroom and sometimes walking out. Zaria was aware that Mushana needed to work on communication and cooperative learning and that this was difficult for him.

Zaria sat down and discussed her concerns around the challenges and her frustrations when working with Mushana with her class teacher. She admitted that she was beginning to lose confidence in herself and was becoming a little anxious when she knew she was going to be working with this particular group. The class teacher and Zaria decided to unpick the issues a little more, and the class teacher gave Zaria reassurance that she also had challenges with Mushana, and maybe it was a good moment to reflect on what was working, what wasn't going so well, what could be the triggers, and whether there were other ways to be doing things which might have a better outcome for everyone.

Firstly, and very importantly, they spoke with Mushana to find out his perspective on how he felt about doing group work. He told them he much preferred to work on his own as he liked to do things in his own way, and other pupils would talk about other things not relating to the work that has been set, and he wanted to stay focused on the task in hand. When he would tell them to stop talking about other things, they would get angry with him and they would do it more.

Zaria and the teacher looked at the group work coming up for the following week. They looked at the objectives for the lessons, Mushana's targets on his EHCP and the type of activities that were incorporated for the week. They took each one in turn and broke them down into focusing on which targets or objectives they would be working on with Mushana and what were the best strategies to be doing this.

For one activity, it was decided that Mushana needed to focus on the maths curriculum work, so although he would be working at the group table so that he could be supported if needed and directed to the use of resources, he would be able to work alone for this. Within an English lesson, it was decided that Zaria would try a think–pair–share approach to generating ideas, verbalising them with a partner and then sharing with Zaria. Finally, within a science activity they decided to do a whole group activity but allocating pupils with a clearly defined role within the group so that they took responsibility for an area of the group work. Within the group there were equipment monitors (collecting, cleaning and returning equipment), a data monitor (collecting and recording the data), a practical experiment part 1 administrator, a practical experiment part 2 administrator and a note taker. Zaria spoke with Mushana before the lesson and prepared him for the activity. On this occasion, she asked whether he preferred a particular role (with the idea that over the course of a half term, each of the pupils in the group would rotate around the roles). Mushana chose to be a data collector.

The week went much more smoothly. The maths group work went well, and Mushana was more relaxed working on his own with some support, while Zaria led the rest of the group. The English group work worked better as a pair rather than the whole group as Zaria was able to move the pair on more quickly too, rather than waiting for the contributions from the whole group, and although the science experiment was very active and there were still some issues around sensory needs and noise levels, Mushana was very focused on his role and enjoyed doing this.

Zaria and the class teacher decided to review the group work at the beginning of each week and look at the objectives and targets to see what would be best for Mushana on a weekly basis.

Reflect

Zaria had used the allocation of specific roles for the science activity; how well do you think this type of activity might transfer across subjects? What subjects might it work best in, and which subjects might it be more difficult to apply it in?

Activity

Speak with your class teacher, mentor or line manager, and see if you are able to observe group work happening in other classes with experienced TAs/LSAs. It could be for short periods of time of 15–20 minutes. What do they do that is similar to you? What do they do that is different? Is there anything that you could take away to incorporate within your own practice?

Professional Discussion

Discuss with your class teacher and other TAs and LSAs what strategies and activities make group work successful for them when working with neurodivergent pupils. Is there anything that is working well for you when you are working with a group of neurodivergent pupils? Can you share this with your peers?

Working with Neurodivergent Pupils Implementing Specific Intervention Programmes

There are many types of intervention programmes that may be happening in your schools. Here is an overview of some of the interventions that may be taking place.

Behaviour Interventions

Behaviour interventions are normally carried out when a pupil is having difficulty regulating emotions and presenting with challenging behaviour. They may have an EHCP and a target about managing their behaviour too. A member of support staff could carry out intervention work relating to specific strategies for a pupil to recognise when they are beginning to dysregulate and when emotions are becoming unmanageable and therefore affecting the outward behaviour then seen in the classroom. The TA/LSA should be trained in working with the pupil on strategies, and a support plan be put into place that gives clear guidance on the process and strategies to be used. It is always important to remember that for the behaviour seen, there is an underlying issue or barrier that needs to be investigated or addressed too.

Collaborative Interventions

Group interventions will enable groups of pupils to rehearse subject content and knowledge through group discussions and team work. Pupils will be given the opportunity to listen to the contribution of other pupils which can help them to generate or confirm their own ideas or to challenge their thoughts and develop new thinking around a topic or area of discussion.

Group interventions will be delivering a specific programme based around gaps in curriculum knowledge and skills rather than general group work as seen in the above sections earlier in the chapter. As we know, group work can pose difficulties for some of our neurodivergent pupils, and this must be considered when implementing collaborative interventions.

One-to-One Intervention

As you will see from the next section, the EEF (2021) endorses the use of one-to-one targeted and specific interventions for pupils as being the best way to gain progress in curriculum outcomes.

This targeted support identifies specific areas of content knowledge and skills in which a pupil has gaps in. These interventions provide the opportunity for a pupil to work directly and individually with a TA or LSA on very personalised targets, and there is greater scope and achievement of accelerated learning via one-to-one interventions. These types of interventions are normally implemented in short bursts of approximately 20 minutes a session with several sessions a week.

Classroom-Based Interventions

Classroom-based interventions can be an effective strategy to support the development of pupils in a structured way without being removed from the class base. This can have positive effects on pupils as they are not seen as being singled out for additional support in the same way when they are removed from the class. It also minimises disruption for the pupils as part of their day. As you will see, this has benefits for neurodivergent pupils as they will be staying in the same environment with less change. However, distraction from other pupils and other teaching that may be happening at the same time will need to be considered. Pre-teaching as seen in Chapter 6 could occur as a classroom-based intervention.

Social, Emotional and Well-Being Interventions

Some interventions will not be based on academic progress and will be centred around pupils' social, emotional health and well-being, which are just as important. Some pupils may have experienced trauma or loss, and intervention groups within schools for group of pupils may be held. It is a safe space for pupils to explore their thoughts and feelings and share experiences with pupils and adults. These groups may include a grief or loss group, a nurture group, an exam anxiety group or a communication skills group. These are just a few examples.

Activity

Find out what intervention and support groups are taking place within your school that centre around the social, emotional and well-being aspects for your pupils? How do pupils access these? How are they referred to these groups? Is there a waiting list? Are you able to observe what some of these groups look like, and are there any skills from these groups that can be transferred back into the classroom?

Peer Tutoring

Peer tutoring is more common in secondary school settings. This is when a more experienced peer buddies up with a less experienced peer to provide some tutoring and support in a specific area of development. Both the peer tutor and the tutee will benefit from this, developing their own personal skills. A peer tutoring programme will need to be facilitated and overseen by a support member of staff, with progress being monitored and the match between the peer tutor and tutee observed to ensure that any difficulties are worked through. There are many benefits of peer tutoring for neurodivergent pupils. Often neurodivergent pupils prefer to work with an adult rather than their peers, as they feel safer with direction from an adult. Peer tutoring can bridge this gap with a mentor that is experienced, and often a little older than themselves.

Metacognition and Self-Regulation Interventions

Intervention programmes that focus on metacognition and self-regulation focus on pupils thinking about their own learning. We know how important this is from earlier chapters. This type of programme might focus on specific areas such as self-management, evaluation of work, setting goals for themselves, monitoring your own progress and motivating your own learning.

Implementing specific intervention programmes is different to working one-to-one with pupils. Although it could be that you are working on a one-to-one basis with a pupil on an intervention programme or as part of a small group.

The EEF (2021) has an online toolkit for working with pupils on a one-to-one basis and implementing specific targeted interventions and tuition. Its research focus is based upon interventions that are being delivered to develop curriculum knowledge and skills rather than interventions around social and emotional and well-being, for example. Their key findings show:

1   On average, one-to one tuition is very effective at improving pupil outcomes. One-to-one tuition might be an effective strategy for providing targeted support for pupils who are identified as having low prior attainment or are struggling in particular areas.
2   Tuition is more likely to make an impact if it is additional to, and explicitly linked with, normal lessons.
3   One-to-one tuition can be expensive to deliver, particularly when delivered by teachers. Approaches that deliver instruction through teaching assistants or in small groups rather than one-to-one have smaller positive effects, on average, but may be a cost-effective solution to providing targeted support.

4 For one-to-one tuition led by teaching assistants, interventions are likely to be particularly beneficial when the teaching assistants are experienced, well trained and supported – for example, delivering a structure intervention.

(EEF, 2021)

The EEF (2021) outlines that to implement this individual support in schools effectively, the following should happen:

- The accurate identification of the pupils that need the additional support. This could be done through the graduated approach, and pupils would be identified by the class teacher and the SENCo.
- The understanding of the learning gaps that each individual pupil has, and that the additional tuition is applied to address these gaps in curriculum knowledge and content.
- Ensure that the deliverer of the intervention is well prepared and having high-quality interactions with pupils such as giving well-planned feedback.
- Assessment from this should then be given to the class teacher on pupils' progress, and the tuition then needs adjusting accordingly to the needs of the pupil.
- One-to-one tuition should be well linked to the classroom content and must allow time for the teacher and the tutor to discuss the tuition so that these links can be made. This will ensure the knowledge and skills are being transferred from the tuition back into the classroom and across curriculum content and subjects.
- The one-to-one tuition may be delivered by teachers, trained teaching assistants, academic mentors or tutors. Interventions are typically delivered over an extended period of time, often over several weeks or a term.

Implementing an Intervention

When you are asked to run an intervention group, ensure that you have been trained in the intervention programme itself and that you understand the requirements of the programme and the aims.

Ensure that you know:

- If you are running a group intervention, which pupils will be in the group, what are their needs, and what individual knowledge do you need to know about each of them? Is there anything regarding their neurodivergent needs that you need additional information on? For example, do any pupils have sensory needs or have anxiety about change?
- Why does each of the pupils have been chosen for the intervention? What do you need to know about the gaps in their knowledge or skills?
- What is the specific focus of the intervention programme?

- How many sessions are included for the programme? Is there any flexibility to extend the programme or to move the programme on more quickly if need be? If so, how will you prepare your neurodivergent pupils for this?
- How long will the sessions last, and how frequent are they?
- What are the measurable outcomes against the objectives, and how will this be recorded and reported back, and to whom?
- What will the sessions look like? Will resources be needed? Will these be provided or will you need to make any resources in advance? Will any additional resources be needed for the specific needs of your neurodivergent pupils?
- Where will the sessions take place? Within the classroom, in a base room or in corridor? Think about what this might mean for your neurodivergent pupils with sensory needs and possible distractions.
- Are there specific tests or exams that pupils are working towards that you will need to be linking in to?
- If there is anything that is unclear, check in with your class teacher or the SENCo before you start the intervention or as you progress through it.

Managing Time When Delivering Interventions

Managing time within delivering intervention programmes can be tricky. You will have a set programme that will need to be delivered in a particular way, with specific content delivered, and a set number of sessions and timings. So how can you manage this?

- Check out whether there is flexibility within the programme. Are there opportunities to extend the time for pupils to revisit elements you think that a pupil needs this, or is this built into the programme?
- Is there the opportunity within the programme to move pupils on faster if you think that they have grasped the element that you are working on, or do you need to work through each and every step methodically? It is important to know and understand these elements as they will have been tried and tested, and whatever the format is, it will be the most likely to bring the most success to the pupil outcomes; therefore, you must implement it in the way it has been set out for you.
- If you are working within a group, is the size of the group manageable with the needs of your neurodivergent pupils considered?
- Will there be additional distractions that may take up some of your allocated time? How will you account for this, and what can you do to improve this?
- If you are having difficulty managing the time element of delivering the interventions, who will you be able to discuss this with to make changes to how you are running the programme?

Professional Discussion

Discuss with your SENCo what interventions take place in your school, who implements them and how they are trained in delivering these interventions.

Consider whether this is an area of practice that you may like to develop further, and discuss this with your SENCo.

School Intervention Policies

Some schools may have a specific intervention policy. Check and see whether your school has a separate policy or whether intervention is included as part of another policy such as the special educational needs and disabilities (SEND), curriculum or assessment policy. How is this being implemented in your school? Can you see the policy happening in practice?

The policy could include elements such as:

Aims

- To describe the processes and structure existing within the school which enable learners' gaps to be tackled at every level.
- To outline the role of the Intervention Team to ensure that they support effectively to help to close the pupils' gaps in knowledge and skills.
- To ensure gaps are identified quickly with appropriate intervention being applied to ensure that success and achievement are re-established.

Objectives

- To ensure staff are aware of their role and responsibilities towards supporting the closing of gaps both within discrete subject areas and across the curriculum.
- To adopt a consistent approach to the identification of gaps in knowledge and skills.
- To establish clear processes by which intervention will take place and how it will be evaluated/recorded.

The policy may outline key types of intervention for example:

- Subject-specific interventions – run by the Head of Department or Subject Leader.
- Learning support – run by the SEND department.

- Intervention tuition – Small Group/One-to-One work run as, for example, an eight-session block over four weeks for students who are not progressing as quickly as their peers and run by the Subject Leader.
- Pastoral support – run by the Pastoral Lead.

The policy should outline what interventions can and cannot achieve, for example:

Intervention is NOT meant to replace the work of the teachers in the classroom but to accelerate progress of identified pupils towards the expected levels of achievement. Staff should always be meeting the needs of all the students in their classroom in each lesson, and consequently appropriate support should also be given within lessons. Teachers should not rely on the intervention sessions to do their current work, as the support will be about strengthening skills which have already been identified as limiting progress.

By the end of the eight sessions, the pupils should be able to work effectively in the areas initially identified by the Subject Leaders. Extension work may be set if the pupil makes better than expected progress over the sessions. If a pupil does not make progress, they will be referred back to the Subject Leader who will then consider what further forms of intervention or strategies may be provided for the pupil.

Chapter Summary

This chapter has considered the role of the TA or LSA in relation to working on a one-to-one basis with pupils, the challenges of group work and implementing specific intervention strategies with pupils and the additional considerations needed for working with neurodivergent pupils.

Consider the next steps you would like to make or additional professional development you would like to undertake to progress your own practice in relationship to each of these elements.

Further Reading

- Education Endowment Foundation (2018) Making Best Use of Teaching Assistants. https://educationendowmentfoundation.org.uk/education-evidence/guidance-reports/teaching-assistants?utm_source=/education-evidence/guidance-reports/teaching-assistants&utm_medium=search&utm_campaign=site_searchh&search_term [date accesses 24.07.2022].
- Education Endowment Foundation (2021) One to One Tuition. https://educationendowmentfoundation.org.uk/education-evidence/teaching-learning-toolkit/one-to-one-tuition.
- Iris Connect, How I Support SEND Pupils. https://blog.irisconnect.com/uk/send-teaching.
- Kagan Cooperative Learning Structures. https://education.wm.edu/centers/sli/events/ESL%20101/kagan-cl-structures.pdf.

- Kagan, It's All about Engagement. https://www.kaganonline.com/free_articles/dr_spencer_kagan/264/The-quot-E-quot-of-PIES.
- Reading Rockets. https://www.readingrockets.org/strategies/think-pair-share.

References

Education Endowment Foundation (2018) Making Best Use of Teaching Assistants. https://educationendowmentfoundation.org.uk/education-evidence/guidance-reports/teaching-assistants?utm_source=/education-evidence/guidance-reports/teaching-assistants&utm_medium=search&utm_campaign=site_searchh&search_term [date accesses 24.07.2022].
Education Endowment Foundation (2021) One to One Tuition. https://educationendowmentfoundation.org.uk/education-evidence/teaching-learning-toolkit/one-to-one-tuition.

Reflect

What challenges are you currently facing when working with groups of pupils? Have you had the opportunity to try out some strategies from Chapter 7? What was effective, what wasn't and why do you think this was? What are you going to try next?

8 Working Collaboratively

Chapter Aims

- To gain an understanding of working with the class teacher to support neurodivergent pupils.
- To consider approaches to working with parents and carers of neurodivergent pupils in a learning support assistant (LSA)/ teaching assistant (TA) role.
- To gain an overview of the different roles in education that work together to support neurodivergent pupils.
- To understand that collaborative working is key in supporting neurodivergent pupils.

Links to the Professional Standards for Teaching Assistants

Personal and Professional Conduct

- **1 Having proper and professional regard for the ethos, policies and practices of the school** in which they work as professional members of staff.
- **2 Demonstrating positive attitudes, values and behaviours** to develop and sustain effective relationships with the school community.
- **3 Having regard for the need to safeguard pupils' wellbeing** by following relevant statutory guidance along with school policies and practice.

Knowledge and Understanding

- **2 Demonstrate expertise and skills in understanding the needs of all pupils** (including specialist expertise as appropriate) and know how to adapt and deliver support to meet individual needs.
- **5 Understand their roles and responsibilities within the classroom and whole school context** recognising that these may extend beyond a direct support role.

DOI: 10.4324/9781003427599-9

Working with Others

- **1 Recognise and respect the role and contribution of other professionals, parents and carers** by liaising effectively and working in partnership with them.
- **2 With the class teacher, keep other professionals accurately informed** of progress or concerns they may have about the pupils they work with.
- **3 Understand their responsibility to share** knowledge to inform planning and decision-making.
- **4 Understand their role** in order to be able to work collaboratively with classroom teachers and other colleagues, including specialist advisory teachers.
- **5 Communicate their knowledge and understanding of pupils** to other school staff and education, health and social care professionals so that informed decision-making can take place on intervention and provision.

Introduction

Effective collaborative working is vital in education and for neurodivergent pupils to make progress. However, in a busy school, with a range of professionals to work with, this can be very difficult for everyone. Difficulties include the coordination of services and support, effective use of resources and primarily good communication.

Your neurodivergent pupils will be at the heart of the collaboration that is needed, support from specialists will be drawn upon and you, as a member of support staff, may be the one implementing this support and advice that has been given.

This chapter will give you an overview of some of the professionals and specialists that could be working with your pupils at any given time, and it will give guidance on how to work with colleagues and your class teacher so that you can give the best support to your pupils.

Working with the Class Teacher(s)

As a TA or LSA you will be working with either one class teacher or many class teachers. This will vary from school to school, whether you are assigned to particular pupils or classes, or departments and across year groups and key stages. Your role as a TA or LSA may change and develop over time, and you will work with different teachers and different pupils each year. You will need to develop relationships with a range of professionals as you move through each of these phases of your work.

You will find that some teachers will have a great deal of experience, and some will have less experience and may be an Early Career Teacher (ECT).

Therefore, some teachers will have a particular way of working with their support staff, some may like to give lots of direction and clear guidance and others will be developing their confidence and experience with this. This, of course, will depend upon your own experience too. Some LSAs and TAs have a great deal of experience in the classroom and may need less guidance on implementing strategies and teaching methods, and others may be new to the profession and need clearer direction and modelling themselves by teachers to implement the strategies and support for pupils.

So, what is the best way for you to work with your class teacher(s) when you are supporting neurodivergent pupils?

Your relation with your teacher(s) is possibly one of the most important relationships in education for your neurodivergent pupils. Clear communication around the needs of your pupils, next steps in learning, support strategies and key teaching methods is key in furthering progress. You have already seen many of these strategies in the previous chapters of this book, and this section focuses on communication of those strategies.

Reflect

Make a note of how many classes you work within during a week. How many teachers do you work with? Does this include working with supply or cover teachers when needed? Reflect on your relationships with your teaching colleagues: what works well, and what do you find most challenging about these relationships? Does this have an impact on how you work with your pupils?

How are you used as a TA/LSA? What does your role look like? Do all TAs/LSAs in your school work like this and do similar tasks? Do you think this is effective in supporting your neurodivergent pupils?

We are going to have a look at some research around the use of TAs in school, at what is effective, what is not, and why. You can then consider this against your reflections around your own role and the sort of work that you are currently doing.

Webster, Blatchford and Russell (2013) carried out some research looking at the effective use of TAs in schools. They concluded that depending upon how TAs were used it was vital in securing progress for pupils. They stated that from their research, they found that it was effective for TAs to deliver specific targeted and focused interventions for pupils, and it was not effective for TAs to take and cover whole classes.

- The Education Endowment Foundation (EEF) (2018) which is Continuing Professional Development (CPD).
- TAs do not always get an induction into their role.

- TAs were good at supporting motivation, confidence and self-esteem in pupils.
- TAs eased workload for teachers.

So, what do some of these findings mean? In many schools, LSAs/TAs may have been assigned to work with one pupil. This can have an effect that the particular child becomes reliant on the key person to support them, and there is less opportunity for them to develop independence. It also causes difficulty if the key person is away and can have an impact on a pupil's behaviour. It might be that an Education, Health and Care Plan (EHCP) states that a pupil should have one-to-one support, but what this looks like might vary. It could be that a pupil has several one-to-one members of support staff working with them across the course of a week, and ideally those staff members may be offering hover support, checking in with the pupil and allowing for times of independence. The use of modelling and scaffolding is particularly important here, and it will vary from task to task and subject to subject.

It is known that TAs and LSAs have little opportunity to participate in training and CPD. This is normally due to many reasons including school budgets and contracts employing support staff from 8:45 am until 3:00 pm, rather than having additional time for training. It could also be that the staff member can't attend training after or before school because they need to take their own children to school or pick them up. However, many schools are now moving towards working out ways in which TAs and LSAs can gain training and CPD. It could include time during school assemblies or online training. Much of the time though, it will be your class teacher that works with you to help you develop your skills and knowledge to support your neurodivergent pupils, which is why this book is important to give you grounding and understanding of some of the skills and strategies that you could implement.

As you have previously read, the EEF (2018) clearly outlines recommendations on how best support staff should be used within schools. The 'Further Reading' section at the end of the chapter details this, but the recommendations are summarised below:

1 Support staff should not be used as an informal teaching resource for only the low attaining pupils.
2 Support staff need to add value to what teachers do, not be used to replace teachers.
3 Support staff need to be used to help pupils develop independent learning skills (as seen in previous chapters) and manage their own learning.
4 Support staff must be fully prepared for their role in the classroom.
5 Support staff can be used to deliver high-quality interventions on a one-to-one basis and small group support.
6 Evidence-based interventions should be used by support staff.
7 Explicit connections should be made between the interventions and everyday classroom teaching and learning.

The next section will consider each of these in turn and what they will look like in your role and for your neurodivergent pupils.

1 Support staff should not be used as an informal teaching resource for only the low attaining pupils.

How are you deployed within your classroom or across classes? Are you allocated to work with a particular pupil? Do you always work with your neurodivergent pupils, or do you work across all the pupils within your class(es)? Do you see a range of pupil needs and attainment?

Case Study

From an LSA: What Works Best When Working with a Teacher and a Neurodivergent Pupil

I am an experienced LSA and I have worked with around ten teachers in the time that I have been an LSA. Each year, there is always a new way of working, or a different way depending upon the new teacher that I am working with. At times it can be tricky getting to know how they work, or what their expectations are, and even how organised they are! Developing a trusting relationship with them is key. I need to be able to say to them if I don't understand something they ask me to do, or how to implement a strategy so that they can show me.

For me, the way I like to work best is to have a good overview of the whole class. This normally happens more at the beginning of the year when the teacher is getting to know them too. So rather than working with just one group of pupils, for example, the neurodiverse group or SEND group, I work with a different group on each day across the week. This gives me an initial understanding of what the attainment levels the pupils are working at, and a good range of strategies that I can then implement and use across the class.

Working in this way also means that the class teacher also works with all of the pupils, including the neurodivergent pupils. What I like about this, is that I can then draw upon the experience of the teacher, we can have discussions around what has worked for them, or what to avoid! I can mirror the behaviour strategies so that we are consistent, and I can use the teaching strategies that they have modelled.

What I find most difficult is not having access to the training that I would like to do. I want to get better at supporting pupils and be up to date with what I should be implementing, but I have my own children to pick up from school, the dinner to make etc, and there is just never enough time to do all of this. I currently have a good teacher that I am working with though, and they spend the time feeding back to me on any training that they have had within their staff meetings, or they will bring me some reading and make time within class for me to read through this, and think how I might incorporate it when I am working with my pupils.

2 *Support staff need to add value to what teachers do, not be used to replace teachers.*

This reflects upon the case study above, all pupils should have time with their class teacher, and neurodivergent pupils should be working with their teacher too, not working solely working with a TA or LSA. Support staff should not be used to cover classes either unless they have been trained to do so, and have gained the specific skills and knowledge to do this.

3 *Support staff need to be used to help pupils develop independent learning skills (as seen in previous chapters) and manage their own learning.*

This draws upon many aspects from previous chapters in the book. It includes the use of scaffolding support for pupils, using adaptive teaching methods, and the development of independent skills to work in the classroom. Support staff need to develop their skills in supporting pupils' skill development, rather than focussing on the completion of tasks that have been set for them. For example, rather than a pupil answer all of the questions on a maths sheet which has been heavily supported by an LSA, it is better for a pupil to complete less questions, but be embedding the skills and knowledge of how to do this, and be able to retrieve this information so that they can work independently to do it the following time. This draws upon what we know about metacognition and retrieval practice.

4 *Support staff must be fully prepared for their role in the classroom.*

Communication is key, so that a TA or LSA knows what to do within a lesson and how. For some of you, this may be even more difficult if you work in a secondary school and work with many different teachers across a range of departments. You may need to think about whether communication is effective, and if not, is it having an impact on your neurodivergent pupils?

Reflect

Consider how information is given to you regarding a lesson, who you are going to work with, what the lesson content is, what subject knowledge you will need to have, and what teaching strategies you will need to use.

Are you given a lesson plan? Does this contain instructions or direction for yourself? Do you have a discussion with the class teacher at the start of the day or before the lesson? Or do you have to try and follow the lesson as it is taught and pick it up as you go along?

This might be an area of discussion to take forward with your class teacher: do you feel prepared to teach your individuals or groups based on the information that you are given, or would you benefit from having this information in another form so that you can impact on pupil learning further?

5 *Support staff can be used to deliver high-quality interventions on a one-to-one basis and small group support.*

TAs and LSA will need specific training on specific interventions to be able to deliver them effectively. This may be an area in which you would like to develop further on so that you can work with pupils across the school and age ranges and become an expert in a particular subject area or intervention for your pupils. This has been discussed in detail in Chapter 7.

Activity

What range of interventions are delivered within your school? If you are not sure, find out from your class teacher or Special Educational Needs Co-ordinator (SENCo). Do you currently deliver any interventions? What training have you had on these? Has it been adequate?

If not, who will you approach to discuss whether further training might be beneficial? Are there any interventions that you are interested in delivering within your school, and how can you gain training on these?

---

6 *Evidence-based interventions should be used by support staff.*

Interventions that are delivered should be chosen because the evidence-base shows that they are effective and have an impact on pupil progress. Intervention sessions should be short in length but happen regularly, for example, several times a week. Assessment of the impact of the intervention should take place for each pupil as part of the cycle of the graduated approach. This has been discussed in detail in Chapter 7.

7 *Explicit connections should be made between the interventions and everyday classroom teaching and learning.*

It is also important that if you are carrying out the intervention and that you discuss what this is and how it works with the pupil's support staff in the classroom so that they can make links between the intervention and their daily classroom learning, in order to practise and embed the skills and knowledge.

Working with Parents and Carers

Although it is the role of the teacher to work directly with parents and carers, often in primary schools it can be an LSA or TA who has some contact with them. This is particularly true at the start or the end of a day when settling a child in or catching up with a parent or carer on how the day has been. Although it is less often that you would work with parents and carers in a secondary school, it does happen, particularly when you are working with neurodivergent pupils as you may be meeting up with them to take messages, or again to report back on how something has gone as you have been the main person working with them.

Building positive relationships is vital, and it can be difficult. Parents and carers may see things differently to how you see them in the classroom; for example, a pupil may be trying to hold everything in all day at school or masking their anxiety, but when they return to the comfort and safety of the home environment, they let this mask down and the frustration and the pressure of the day are let out resulting in challenging behaviours. Or it could be the opposite way around, and the pupil could be exhibiting challenging behaviour at school from the sensory overload that they are experiencing constantly, but the parent or carer doesn't see this at home because the child returns to the comfort and safety of home and relaxes.

Drawing out information from parents can be very beneficial for you to see what works with them at home to engage a pupil who you can then replicate in class, and again can be a two-way process in which you may give examples to parents on what might be working well in school.

Case Study

From the Parent of a Neurodivergent PupilWhat Works Best When Working with Parents

At times I find it really difficult as a parent of a neurodivergent child. I have lots of on-going worries and questions that can't be answered, such as what the future might hold for them? Or how will they cope being an adult? These questions can sometimes overshadow the day-to-day challenges, and everything can feel a bit overwhelming.

For me, as a parent, what has worked well in schools is being told all of the good things that happen! So often I am focused on the negatives and how to change and improve things; it is really good to hear the positives, and there are normally lots of them, but with some teachers, I am only told the negatives. With the teachers who tell me the positives, I no longer dread seeing the school number flash up on my phone, as, more often than not, it is to tell me something that has gone really well.

Developing a trusting relationship where I don't feel judged for being a bad parent has made me more open to talking with staff about what might be happening at home. Sometimes I used to not want to tell anyone if we had had a bad evening or morning, because I would think that the school would think it was all my fault. But I now know that the staff who work with my child have a good understanding of neurodivergent needs and are not judging me, but looking at ways to support me and my child instead.

Occasionally, things haven't gone so well, but this has been around trying to access services, or paperwork not being completed, or staff just being too busy. For me though, my child comes first, and I expect this from others too, so this is when I become a bit frustrated.

Billington (2019) agrees with how parent's feel, daily challenges, frustration and isolation can become part of their identity. She states that parental experiences show that they feel as though they are always fighting for their children: fighting for a diagnosis, fighting for support and fighting for not feeling judged. It is really important to support parents through keeping an open dialogue and to move away from 'a hostile and judgemental societal view of developmental differences in children'.

Some strategies for developing communication with parents and carers include:

- Be open with your communication. Develop a trusting relationship so that parents and carers feel as though they can tell you about the challenges that they are facing, or if they have any worries or concerns.
- Ensure that you focus on the positives of the neurodiversity model. Discuss and feed back on what is going well.
- Find out what strategies work well for the parents or at home. Improving consistency across settings also helps.
- Parents or carers may be very well educated around the needs of their child; they may have attended training courses or read extensively around the subject. Enable them to share this understanding and don't be afraid to let them know that they know more than you and draw on their advice and support or direction for further training for yourself.
- In other cases, you may know more than the parent or carer; however, do not try and diagnose a pupil, as that is not your job or expertise, and do not contradict a diagnosis that has been given by a professional in the field. The pupil will have undergone a rigorous assessment procedure, and although you may not have seen all of the elements for a diagnosis, then the assessment team will have.
- At the end of this chapter, there is a section on the use of professional language. Never use inappropriate language about a child or joke with a parent about a label or diagnosis.

Working with Education Professionals

There are many educational professionals that work with neurodivergent pupils. This section will look at the range of professionals who may be working with your pupils. Although you may not have direct contact with these professionals, the advice and strategies that they give or the work that they do will have a direct impact on what you are doing.

Reflect

What Educational professionals are you aware of that work with your neurodivergent pupils? What type of work do they do?

- Behaviour support advisors –behaviour support advisors are employed by the Local Authority and work with schools on strategies to support pupils with challenging behaviours.
- Behaviour support home workers – behaviour support home workers work closely with the behaviour support advisors and work with parents and carers in the home to join up the thinking and support across the settings.
- SENCo – you will have a SENCo in your school. In very small primary schools, this might be a dual role with the headteacher or deputy headteacher, or it might be a part-time role. In secondary schools, there may be a special educational needs and disabilities (SEND) team with a SENCo, assistant SENCo and support workers.
- Child and Adult Mental Health Services (CAMHS) team – CAMHS may work with pupils to overcome trauma, anxiety or depression. They may hold group or individual sessions. Normally a pupil is referred to CAMHS and will be given a set number of sessions to attend. Progress is monitored during this time and the impact of the sessions reviewed.
- Educational psychologist (EP) – an EP will assess a pupil through carrying out a variety of cognitive tests. The results of these will help to build a picture of the pupil's strengths and areas of difficulty. An EP will conduct an assessment and write a report if the school is gathering evidence for an EHCP application. Schools are allocated a number of sessions from EPs each year, and often this is not enough for the number of pupils that the school would like to be seen; therefore, there can be a considerable waiting list to be seen by an EP. The EP will conclude with suggested strategies and resources to support a pupil.
- Education welfare officer (EWO) – an EWO is responsible for monitoring attendance within school. You may be working with a neurodivergent pupil that is having difficulty attending school for a variety of reasons as seen in an earlier case study in Chapter 2, when the pupil was experiencing difficulties with sensory issues. The EWO will work with the school and with parents and carers to improve the attendance of pupils.
- Family liaison officers – family liaison officers will work with families on a particular area of need, such as getting families back into work or supporting housing or financial advice and guidance.

- Specialist teachers – there are specialist teachers in many areas of neurodivergence. They will work with pupils across a geographical area to support progress in school. Their specialism may be in autism; attention-deficit hyperactivity disorder (ADHD); cognitive communication or sensory impairments; or hearing or visual impairments. See what areas are covered by your Local Authority.
- Speech and language therapists – pupils may attend sessions within schools or outside of school with a therapist.
- Social worker – a family or pupil may be working with a social worker who will be monitoring and supporting the safeguarding of a pupil.
- Virtual headteacher – this is a headteacher who oversees all of the Looked After Pupils (LACs) in the area. Many LACs are neurodivergent, and you may be working with pupils that are also in care.

These roles may have different titles or job roles depending on how they are set out within your Local Authority. Compare the list to the list that you made within your reflection on the professionals that you have worked with. Are there any additional professionals to add to the list above?

Multi-agency meetings may be held for a pupil when multiple professionals are working with them. This is an opportunity to draw together all of the strategies and support that is in place and to discuss the progress being made, what is working well and what areas need support next. If a professional cannot attend the meeting, then they will send in a report instead.

Your neurodivergent pupil may also be working with medical professionals who may also attend the multi-agency meeting.

Working with Medical Professionals

There are a range of medical professionals that could also be working with your neurodivergent pupil, including:

- CAMHs – as outlined in the above section.
- Consultant – your neurodivergent pupil may have been referred by a General Practitioner (GP) or the Paediatrician to a consultant for assessment, tests or ongoing support for a specific condition.
- GP – a GP may be referring in to other services or assessment, or they could be supporting a pupil for mental health needs through medicating co-existing conditions and difficulties such as anxiety.
- Nurse – a nurse may be monitoring or supporting a pupil with co-existing medical needs such as epilepsy or mental health.
- Occupational therapist (OT) – the OT will offer practical support, advice and strategies for physical and cognitive barriers to learning.
- Paediatrician – the paediatrician may be assessing a pupil, or monitoring and reviewing around particular conditions.

Promoting Inclusivity and Neurodiversity in Your Classroom

It is important that positivity around neurodiversity is promoted and that the acceptance of difference with different ways of thinking and being in all areas become the norm and are celebrated, as outlined at the beginning of Chapter 1. As we draw near to the end of the book, think about ways in which you can promote positivity around neuro-differences within your own class(es) and with the pupils that you work with. This could include:

- Discuss with pupils and staff how every person thinks, processes information and works differently.
- Promote that there is no right or wrong way to thinking and learning.
- Ensure your neurodivergent pupils get to experience all subjects to learn about their strengths and interests alongside developing their core skills.
- Include activities for positive mental health and well-being within the teaching and activities that you do with your pupils.
- Use active listening and develop positive relationships with all of your pupils.
- Draw upon the positive attributes and qualities of your neurodivergent learners.
- Support parents and carers to understand a model of difference rather than deficit.
- Challenge negative perceptions, attitudes and language towards neurodivergent learners.

Working Professionally: the Use of Language

It is important to end this book on a section on the professional use of language when working with neurodivergent pupils. There may be times when you will need to challenge the use of inappropriate language that others are using when referring to neurodivergent pupils. Incorrect terminology or dated or derogatory language can be deeply offensive.

The use of the neurodiversity model challenges the deficit model and promotes acceptance, and with that, the use of language is incorporated. Having high regard to your own expectations around the use of language is important, and you should use this both within and outside of the classroom.

There is a useful document produced by the Government of Canada (2013) in which they challenge they use of outdated and disrespectful language and offer alternative acceptable ways to describe the challenges that people face. It is a good document to print out or to make into a poster. The Government of Canada (2013) states that 'attitudes can be the most difficult barrier people with disabilities face in achieving full integration, acceptance and participation in society'. It argues that 'we should all put great thought into how we present information about people with disabilities, to help overcome negative attitudes and shape positive ones'. The document link is in the 'Further Reading' section at the end of this chapter. There is a table at the end of the document with the suggested replacement language.

Chapter Summary

Working collaboratively with others can be challenging, but in education you will work with a range of educational professionals and you will need to implement strategies and advice that have been given by them for your neurodivergent pupils. You will be a key member of staff to do this, and you hold an important role for you pupils.

You will manage relationships with class teachers, parents and carers and educational professionals, and it is important to do this using correct language and terminology that is in line with a neurodiverse ethos.

Collaboration is at the heart of supporting your neurodivergent pupils in the classroom, the school environment and more widely working with the families. As you move on with your training and development and as you progress with your educational support staff career, it is important to remember that you hold a vital role in developing the future outcomes for your neurodivergent pupils. Embrace neurodiversity and be advocates for your neurodivergent pupils, by learning more and challenging others to do the same.

Reflect

Reflect back on what you have learnt on supporting neurodivergent pupils in the classroom.

Chapter 1 – Introduction to Neurodiversity, What is Neurodiversity?

You have considered a neurodiverse world in which every brain is different. You have been introduced to the terminology, models used, and the importance of a model of difference rather than deficit.

You have an overview to refer back to of varying neurodiverse labels/diagnoses and languages used: autism (autism spectrum disorder/autism spectrum condition), ADHD, dyslexia, dyscalculia, dyspraxia, Tourette syndrome, pathological demand avoidance, developmental language disorder, general anxiety disorder, post-traumatic stress disorder, attachment, oppositional defiant disorder and obsessive-compulsive disorder.

Chapter 2 – The Learning Environment in a Neurodivergent World

This chapter covered consideration of the school environment for different needs. The classroom space was examined to develop understanding for TAs/LSAs on table layouts, access to resources, use of displays and seating arrangements for individual pupils. It also included the challenges for pupils outside the classroom at social times, how pupils may be supported during these times by support staff and how shared spaces can be organised and used as these are spaces commonly used by TAs/LSAs when working with neurodivergent pupils. Sensory issues both inside the classroom and around the school building and communal areas, and how TAs/LSAs can support neurodivergent pupils with this were outlined.

Chapter 3 – Behaviour Management and Neurodivergent Pupils

This chapter gave guidance on neurodiversity and the behavioural needs of individual pupils, what underlies this behaviour that can cause behavioural challenges for TAs and LSAs and what strategies can support the needs and challenges of the pupils that the support staff may encounter. Behavioural models for support and discussion around school behavioural policies and the needs of neurodivergent pupils were looked at. There was a section on communication such as a breakdown of communication with pupils, processing and language difficulties and different types of communication in school such as written, verbal and visual and how these can cause issues and how they can be used to support pupils.

Chapter 4 – Pupil Well-Being and Neurodiversity

There is a focus on pupil happiness, and this chapter looked specifically at strategies for supporting neurodivergent pupil well-being and anxiety. It looked at common mental health issues such as anxiety and depression in pupils, how this can affect engagement in school and progression within a learning context. Strategies and access to support and further direction for access to additional resources were outlined.

Chapter 5 – Supporting the Assessment Needs of Neurodivergent Pupils

This chapter considered the types of assessment in a school setting. Looking at a range of assessment for learning approaches and summative assessment points, it deconstructed the assessment process and evaluated how neurodivergent pupils fit within this model. The graduated approach and how what you do as a TA/LSA fits into this cycle were explored. The chapter progressed to examine specific needs of pupils, strategies to support assessment and how to access them across both the primary and secondary phases. There was an overview on summative assessment points such as Key Stage Standardised Assessment Tests, General Certificate of Secondary Education and A levels and access arrangements for these that might be supported by the TA/LSA.

Chapter 6 – Supporting Progression of Neurodivergent Pupils

This chapter examined the teaching and learning strategies to support the progression of pupils, outlined specific challenges relating to a range of subject areas and explored more general challenges that cross the subject areas.

There was a focus on memory, metacognition and the use of learning sciences such as retrieval practice, cognitive load theory and spacing to support neurodivergent pupils.

Chapter 7 – Working in Different Formats: One-to-One, Groups and Interventions

This chapter considered the TA/LSA role in working with neurodivergent pupils on a one-to-one basis, managing learning and progression with small group working and delivering a range of interventions. This chapter linked back to previous chapters such as Chapter 3 looking at behaviour management, and Chapters 5 and 6 looking at assessment and strategies for progression. It included a section on managing time and feeding back to the class teacher on pupils' progress and outcomes.

Chapter 8 – Working Collaboratively

This chapter focused on the need for effective collaborative working. It is known that this area can be an issue within education, and yet it is vital for the effective support for neurodivergent pupils. There were focus areas looking at working with the class teacher and parents and carers with an overview of who neurodivergent pupils may also be working with such as education professionals including behaviour support workers, attendance and welfare officers and health professionals such as mental health and medical practitioners. Collaboration is at the heart of supporting pupils in the classroom and the school environment and also with the transition to home.

There was an important section on the use of positive language and addressing and challenging derogatory language.

Best of luck in advocating for the acceptance of difference within your schools and beyond schools within society!

Further Reading

- Department for Education (2014) Professional Standards for Teaching Assistants. https://neu.org.uk/advice/professional-standards-teaching-assistants.
- Education Endowment Foundation (2018) Making Best Use of Teaching Assistants. https://educationendowmentfoundation.org.uk/education-evidence/guidance-reports/teaching-assistants?utm_source=/education-evidence/guidance-reports/teaching-assistants&utm_medium=search&utm_campaign=site_searchh&search_term.
- Education Endowment Foundation (2018) Working with Parents to Support Children's Learning. https://educationendowmentfoundation.org.uk/education-evidence/guidance-reports/supporting-parents.
- Government of Canada (2013) A Way with Words and Images. https://www.canada.ca/en/employment-social-development/programs/disability/arc/words-images.html.
- Ofsted (2021) Research and Analysis; Supporting SEND. https://www.gov.uk/government/publications/supporting-send/supporting-send.

References

Billington, J. in Haywood, M. and Jopling, M. (2019) *Research SEND in Ordinary Classrooms*. John Catt Publishing. Woodbridge.

Education Endowment Foundation (2018) Making Best Use of Teaching Assistants. https://educationendowmentfoundation.org.uk/education-evidence/guidance-reports/teaching-assistants?utm_source=/education-evidence/guidance-reports/teaching-assistants&utm_medium=search&utm_campaign=site_searchh&search_term [date accesses 24.07.2022].

Ofsted (2021) Research and Analysis; Supporting SEND. https://www.gov.uk/government/publications/supporting-send/supporting-send [date accesses 24.07.2022].

Webster, R., Blatchford, P. and Russell, A. (2013) Challenging and Changing How Schools Use Teaching Assistants: Findings from the Effective Deployment of Teaching Assistants Project. *School Leadership and Management*. Vol 33. No. 1. P78–76.

Index

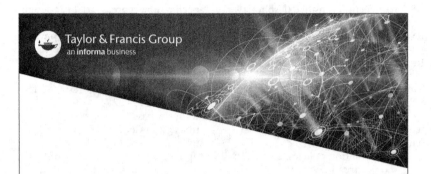

Taylor & Francis eBooks

www.taylorfrancis.com

A single destination for eBooks from Taylor & Francis
with increased functionality and an improved user
experience to meet the needs of our customers.

90,000+ eBooks of award-winning academic content in
Humanities, Social Science, Science, Technology, Engineering,
and Medical written by a global network of editors and authors.

TAYLOR & FRANCIS EBOOKS OFFERS:

A streamlined
experience for
our library
customers

A single point
of discovery
for all of our
eBook content

Improved
search and
discovery of
content at both
book and
chapter level

REQUEST A FREE TRIAL
support@taylorfrancis.com

 Routledge
Taylor & Francis Group

 CRC Press
Taylor & Francis Group

Printed in the United States
by Baker & Taylor Publisher Services